YOUR WELLBEING
BLUEPRINT
FEELING GOOD
AND DOING WELL AT WORK

MICHELLE MCQUAID & DR PEGGY KERN

Your Wellbeing Blueprint: Feeling Good And Doing Well At Work

Authors: Michelle McQuaid and Dr. Peggy Kern

PO Box 230 Albert Park, VIC, 3206 Australia

ABN: 88094250503

www.michellemcquaid.com

Email: chelle@michellemcquaid.com

ISBN: 978-0-9872714-2-6

Editing: Debbie Hindle, Rachel Taylor & Marian Black

Design: Michelle Pirovich www.thesqueezebox.com.au

Typesetting: Michelle Pirovich www.thesqueezebox.com.au

To each of us who want to live in a world where
people genuinely and consistently thrive, and are willing
to do the work to make this a reality.

Contents

Your PERMAH Wellbeing Blueprint

POSITIVE EMOTION	Dialing Up Positivity	Dialing Down Negativity	Practicing Kindness
ENGAGEMENT	Discovering Your Strengths	Creating Moments Of Flow	Developing Your Strengths
RELATIONSHIPS	Investing In Belonging	Creating Purpose	Practicing Storytelling
MEANING	Being Compassionate	Investing In Trust	Giving Effectively
ACCOMPLISHMENT	Setting Goals That Work	Being Hopeful	Practicing a Growth Mindset
HEALTH	Sleeping Well	Eating Wisely	Moving Regularly

Cultivating Gratitude	Savoring The Good	Getting Comfortably Uncomfortable	Short-Circuiting Stress	
Being Mindful	Staying Playful			
Allowing Transcendence	Making Passion Harmonious			
Letting Go & Forgiving	Sharing Good Times	Navigate Incivility		
Developing Grit	Boosting Your Confidence	Embracing Stress	Being Self-Compassionate	Boost Your Resilience
Mindfully Restore				

CHAPTER 1

Feeling Good + Doing Well

The word "wellbeing" gets thrown around a lot. From Aristotle and Buddha to the explosion of the modern self-help movement, history is paved with hundreds of suggestions on how to improve your wellbeing and find happiness. But just what is wellbeing and why might it matter to you, your team, and your workplace?

In its simplest form, wellbeing is your ability to feel good and function effectively. It gives you the resources to navigate the highs and lows that we all experience in our daily lives. It allows you to "be well"—feeling good physically, mentally, emotionally, spiritually, intellectually, and socially— and to "do good"—achieving what you would like to each day, be it at work or at home.

Indeed, studies are finding that high levels of wellbeing relate to all sorts of positive outcomes, including:

- Resilience and energy
- Health and happiness
- Being liked by others
- Productivity and earning more money

Wellbeing certainly sounds like something worth focusing on. Yet, perhaps like us, you've discovered that maintaining your wellbeing is a lot harder than it looks. In fact, a recent study shows that when it comes to our wellbeing, seventy percent of us report spending most of our time somewhere between "functioning" and "flailing." Instead of flourishing, most of us are just trying to get by.

Surely that's just life, right?

By now, we all know that it's important to move regularly, eat wisely, and sleep deeply to stay healthy. But the daily demands of life, unrealistic expectations at work, and even our own sense of worth mean that most of us wind up making choices that undermine our wellbeing. We get it. Despite your best intentions, finding the time and energy to look after yourself is challenging.

But what if it didn't have to be?

What Is Wellbeing?

In 1998, Professor Martin Seligman, who was the president of the American Psychological Association at the time, urged the field of psychology to expand its focus beyond fixing mental illness to promoting sustainable wellbeing. The ideas were nothing new, but Professor Seligman's vision, combined with an era in which people were tired of constant bad news, ignited a fire. The result has been an explosion in our understanding of how people can create and maintain their wellbeing.

Over the past two decades, more than 18,000 peer-reviewed research articles related to wellbeing have been published. Training, certificate, and degree programs have been established online and around the world. Businesses, along with a range of products and services, have been created that aim to help people, organizations, and communities build wellbeing.

Researchers have proposed numerous theories of what wellbeing actually is. In 2011, Professor Seligman offered his own model, known as "PERMA." His model suggests that wellbeing arises from five pillars:

- Positive emotions: experiencing positive feelings such as joy, calmness, and happiness.

- Engagement: being interested and involved in life.

- Relationships: feeling loved, valued, and connected with other people.

- Meaning: having a sense of direction, feeling that our lives are valuable and worthwhile, and connecting to something bigger than ourselves.

- Accomplishment: the belief and ability to do things that matter most to us, achieving goals, and having a sense of mastery.

We (and many others) believe that physical health is also a key part of wellbeing. Everything is just easier when you feel physically healthy. So, we refer to this model as "PERMAH."

To thrive, you need to cultivate each of the PERMAH pillars. How much you'll need of each will vary depending on the type of person you are, the situations you're in, and the outcomes you want to achieve. And you may even find that within each pillar some activities matter more for your wellbeing than others. This means there is no single blueprint for wellbeing. The right plan looks different for each of us.

This is why we've chosen the PERMAH framework to guide the activities, tools and approaches shared in this book, as it provides a framework for thinking about specific, actionable ways that you can build your own wellbeing. We did not choose it because we believe it has been conclusively proven as the roadmap to wellbeing; after all, good science is never proven but is an evolving process of ongoing learning and refinement. Rather, we chose it because we've found that the PERMAH framework is a useful, easy way for people to understand, measure, and take action using evidence-based research and tools.

Can Your Wellbeing Be Improved?

Just like muscle groups and different types of fitness, researchers have found that it is possible to build and improve each of the PERMAH pillars by regularly engaging in wellbeing habits and activities. These activities are known as "Positive Interventions" and include activities like keeping a gratitude journal, breaking the grip of rumination, developing your strengths, finding meaning in small tasks, and overcoming self-doubt.

So does this mean that with the right positive interventions you'll soon be effortlessly flourishing?

Well, not quite.

Researchers believe that your wellbeing—much like your body weight—has a genetically determined set-point range that for most of us is naturally stable and relatively positive. Just as eating well and exercising regularly may help you to maintain or even improve your optimal body weight, the same seems to be true when you consistently engage in practices that support your wellbeing. Unfortunately, this also works in reverse. When you don't eat well or exercise regularly, you're likely to end up weighing more than is ideal for your body type and may even change your set-point over time, making it harder to loose weight. It also appears that when you don't prioritize the practices that support your wellbeing, it becomes increasingly difficult for you to consistently feel good and do well.

We'd love to promise you that simply selecting and practicing a few of the positive interventions from this book for a week would magically guarantee your wellbeing. But the truth is that just like eating one piece of broccoli won't suddenly make you healthy, or going for one twenty-minute run won't suddenly make you fit, neither will briefly trying one positive intervention make you thrive. Maintaining a high level of wellbeing requires consistent practice and learning what works for you—and making it a regular habit.

So does this mean that if you create daily practices of positive interventions and stick with them, you'll always be thriving?

Well, not quite. Feeling good and functioning effectively will ebb and flow, depending on what's happening at work and in your life. Rather than setting the goal of flourishing all the time, we've found that the real prize is in becoming an informed, confident, and active participant in shaping your own wellbeing so you can wholeheartedly show up and be fully engaged in life — whatever it throws at you.

Being an effective steward of your wellbeing is a skill that can be learned and mastered, and ultimately this is what will consistently shape your wellbeing over time.

Moving Toward Wellbeing

So how can you take control of your wellbeing? Depending on what's going on in your life, you might not always feel that you're thriving, but you would still like to know that your wellbeing efforts are making a difference. This means that you need a way to see small signs of success.

Feedback loops are invisible forces that help shape human behavior. They tell us what is working and what is not working, and whether or not we are on track, often in subtle ways. Everyday examples include the number of steps counted on your pedometer, the number of likes on your latest Facebook post, comments during your performance review, or the digital display on the side of the road that registers your speed and tells you to slow down. Feedback loops provide you with a sense of where you are, enabling you to compare this to where you want to be, and giving you the opportunity to adjust your behavior accordingly.

For example, you might step on the bathroom scale to measure your current weight, compare this to your goal weight, and then decide that you want to be mindful about your eating habits and change the amount you exercise. You start eating differently and do more physical activity. Each day, you step onto the bathroom scale to see what impact your efforts are having, and you continue to make adjustments over time.

So how can you create a feedback loop like this that measures your wellbeing?

This is the kind of question that lights Peggy up. Several years ago, she was working as a postdoctoral research fellow at the University of Pennsylvania alongside Professor Seligman. Researchers and policymakers were starting to consider whether people's wellbeing could indeed be measured and monitored. She began to explore whether measuring people's wellbeing— creating a feedback loop around how a person was feeling and functioning— might positively impact the way people behaved.

With the help of Julie Butler, a student in the Masters of Positive Psychology program, the PERMA-Profiler was created. Peggy and Julie compiled hundreds of relevant items that measured emotions, engagement, relationships, meaning, accomplishment, and health. Through a series of studies, they whittled the items down and created twenty-three questions. Tested and validated with tens of thousands of people around the world, the PERMA-Profiler provides a way for people to check how they are doing on each PERMA pillar.

The PERMA-Profiler focuses on your general wellbeing. Peggy subsequently created an alternative measure, which was specifically designed to measure wellbeing at work—the PERMAH Workplace Survey.

We like to think of taking the PERMAH Workplace Survey as the wellbeing equivalent of stepping onto the bathroom scale. The survey only takes a few minutes to complete. It provides an easy way for you to understand how you 're doing in each PERMAH pillar, and compare it to the way you want to be working and the life you want to be living.

The survey is designed to give you a snapshot of where you are right now. It is not meant to be prescriptive. There is no single score that indicates you are thriving. Indeed, what feels like the "right score" for one person may not resonate with another person. Some people may even feel that they've overemphasized one area (e.g., accomplishment) at the expense of another (e.g., relationships). At different times in your career or life, one area might matter far more than another. The survey provides a visual description, so you can make informed choices about what is happening for you now and over time, what is working, and which areas might need a bit more attention.

Just as you can use your bathroom scale to discover how different exercise plans or eating habits impact your weight, the PERMAH Workplace Survey provides a feedback loop to start making more informed and intelligent choices about your wellbeing priorities. It can help you build your own personal wellbeing blueprint to suit the type of person you are, the situations you find yourself in, and the outcomes you most desire.

How Can This Book Help?

If by now you're feeling that improving your wellbeing might be a little harder than you first hoped, you're probably right. There's no quick fix, no silver bullet, no magic pill. In fact, quick fixes might make you feel good in the short term, but can be harmful in the long term.

If you want to be physically strong and fit, simply going to the gym for a day will not be enough. The many machines and exercise options can be pretty overwhelming, and spending a day or two exercising will probably just make you feel sore and tired, not fit and strong. Instead, you'll need to gradually build your fitness over time. You start by assessing your current state of fitness, then set realistic goals for what you'd like to achieve and create a training plan to help you move forward. You might work with a trainer, learning how to use the different machines and which exercises build different muscle groups. You might try out different exercises, finding which ones you like and which ones you never want to do again! You might get a friend to work out with you, providing mutual support and encouragement. And then you reassess your fitness at different times, celebrating your progress and deciding whether to make adjustments to your training plan based on the outcomes you're achieving.

Figuring out how to thrive is no different. This book has been created in the hope that together we can help you create a blueprint for your wellbeing by providing you with easy-to-use tools for measurement, guidance to set effective goals, evidence-based Positive Psychology activities and exercises to guide your practices, and feedback loops to determine what impact your efforts are having on your ability to thrive more consistently.

Here's how to get the most from this "how-to" wellbeing blueprint:

1. **Measure Your Wellbeing**

   Use the free online PERMAH Workplace Survey measure at **www.permahsurvey.com** to get started and see how you're doing in each of the PERMAH pillars right now.

2. **Reflect On Your Wellbeing**

   When you get your results, don't worry about your score. Higher scores are generally better, but the goal is not to be a 10 out of 10 on everything.

   Instead, tune into how you feel about your results. Consider these questions:

   • What does your overall profile look like?

   • Are there some areas that are higher or lower?

   • How do you score on the pillars that are most important to you?

   • Are there areas in which you'd like to see improvement for the life you want to be living?

   • Which PERMAH pillars does this suggest you should prioritize?

3. **Set Your Wellbeing Hopes**

    Of course, it's one thing to know what you feel like you should be doing and another thing to actually find the time and energy to do it. Life is busy, and creating change is challenging—no matter how motivated you are to do so. Having good intentions is not sufficient for creating change.

    Fortunately, research can tell us a lot about trying to change our behavior. First, it is useful to develop specific goals. We often set vague goals like, "I want to be 'healthy' or 'happy.'" It's hard to achieve a goal that is not clearly defined. Guidance on specific strategies to follow and how to know when you actually reach your goal can be helpful.

    This is where the PERMAH framework is useful. Rather than trying to improve your wellbeing, we encourage you to pick a specific area to work on. By targeting different PERMAH pillars at different times, it contributes to your overall sense of wellbeing. If you're not sure where you'd most like to start, each of the following chapters includes an overview of the potential benefits that working on each PERMAH pillar may bring.

    The type of goals you select matter. Researchers have discovered that while eighty-nine percent of us believe that tomorrow will be better than today, only fifty percent of us believe we can make it so. They suggest that the difference is between *wishing* and *hoping*. People who wish expect things to just happen. People who hope set clear "want-to" goals; they try multiple pathways to achieve them, and they ensure up-front that they have ways to maintain their willpower. This is why we recommend that you select the pillars you really "want to" improve, rather than the ones you feel you "should do" or "have to." As you reflect on your profile, what area stands out to you that gets you excited about focusing on it?

A common mistake people make is trying to change too much at once. In trying to be healthier, you might set goals to start working out, eat healthy, sleep more, drink moderately, and stop smoking. That works for the first week, but it quickly becomes overwhelming. Rather than trying to change your whole wellbeing profile at once, it's helpful to pick one or two PERMAH pillars at a time. So, if you could invest your energy in **just** one or two PERMAH pillars right now, which ones would you most like to improve?

We also know that because life is busy, setting small, short-term, manageable goals is more likely to move you toward success than big, long-term goals. You might have a vision of where you want to be in the future, but without specific pathways to get there, it will remain a distant dream. You might try to improve your wellbeing, but have little indication of success, which can be frustrating and demotivating. By focusing on small, achievable goals, you can see change occur and build confidence and momentum along the way. So, as you set up your plan, we recommend focusing on a four-, eight-, or twelve-week time period. Then, measure your wellbeing at the end of this period to see what progress you've made and use this as a feedback loop to set your next goal.

Finally, what's the right time frame for you to really see an improvement in your wellbeing? The more time you spend engaged in an activity, the more it becomes part of who you are and what you do. But, we also have no doubt that you're already living a pretty busy life. In fact, finding the time to prioritize your wellbeing is the biggest obstacle most people face. Based on your life right now, what amount of time and energy is realistic for you to spend on your wellbeing each day? Ten minutes? Half an hour? An hour? Being realistic about your available time will help you select the positive interventions that are most likely to work for you. Fortunately, many of the exercises are simple and only take a few minutes a day. Just as research finds that adding a bit of physical activity throughout the day is beneficial, adding positive behaviors throughout the day can make it more manageable.

4. **Choose Your Wellbeing Intervention**

Once you've selected the PERMAH pillars you'd most like to improve and are clear on the time frame and time commitment you want to work within, turn to the chapter for that pillar and select a positive intervention you'd like to try. Try to choose something that will feel like you're giving yourself a little gift each time you do it. Remember that you might need to experiment with the different exercises to find the ones that suit you.

5. **Create Wellbeing Habits**

Once you've picked an intervention, try to integrate the practice into your everyday actions. The goal is to create simple, positive habits. At first, a new exercise takes energy and effort. It feels awkward and unnatural. But, by practicing an action repeatedly, it becomes easier and more automatic.

One of the challenges of changing behavior is that we have well-ingrained habits, which are often not the best for us. We might need to replace a bad habit with a positive one. But how do we do that?

Habitual behavior is driven in part by reward loops in our brains, which include cues, routines, and rewards. Cues signal the brain that a particular action is required. This often occurs subconsciously, so we may not be aware of our triggers or when they occur. Routines are established behaviors, often associated with a cue. Rewards provide a signal to the brain that the action was good, which reinforces the behavior over time.

For example, you might have a habit of eating ice cream when you watch television. You come home from work, turn on the television, and the next thing you know, you've eaten half a carton of ice cream. The cue is turning on the television, the behavior is eating ice cream, and it triggers the feel-good sensors in the brain, thus rewarding the behavior. These loops can make it challenging to change our behavior, but we can also harness these loops to create a new or preferred habit. Create a habit by choosing:

- **A cue to trigger off the behavior:** You can anchor it in habits you already have, so that one behavior flows seamlessly into the next. You can embed it in your environment, so that the habit becomes automatic. Or, you can use a "when/then" statement to prime your brain, so that at a particular time or occurrence, you know which wellbeing action to take.

- **A routine:** This will be the wellbeing practice you've chosen. Remember, even a ten-minute routine is better than not starting at all.

- **A reward:** Whether it's checking the action off a list, sharing your good news, noting it in a gratitude journal, or making yourself a cup of coffee, rewarding your efforts releases feel-good hormones that help to accelerate and embed habit creation. Over time, you might find the practice just naturally feels good. But early on, some external rewards can help. Don't shortchange yourself by not celebrating what you've done. It will make your wellbeing practices far more enjoyable and likely to stick.

We've placed some suggested wellbeing habits throughout this book that build this neurological habit loop based on research we've conducted around the world.

If you find your wellbeing habit isn't sticking, check that the routine is really something you want to spend your time doing. Just because the activities we've chosen are evidence-based doesn't mean they'll work for everybody. Even the very best studies of human behavior only tell us what works for some of the people, some of the time. So feel free to keep trying new routines until you find ones that help you feel good and do good.

If you like the routine but you're having trouble fitting it in or remembering to do it each day, then play with the cue you're using and see if you can make it easier to get the habit started. Starting early in the day and sticking to a regular time will make this easier. Or, try to increase the reward in the early days. Choose a reward that's so good you will complete the routine just to get to it—the most popular reward we've found people choose is their morning cup of coffee!

If you find that your wellbeing activities or habits work really well for a while, but then start to fizzle out, don't despair. The human brain excels at adapting to our conditions—and unfortunately when it comes to the good things in our lives, we have a tendency to grow bored quickly. When your wellbeing habits or experiences no longer feel enjoyable, energizing, or effective, it's just your brain's way of letting you know it might be time to:

- mix it up (try a different intervention)

- start reminding yourself of why this change mattered to you (make it meaningful)

- dig in for a little more gratitude (remember why you're lucky to be able to do what you're doing)

- make sure you're not comparing yourself to others (don't let ever-increasing expectations undermine your wellbeing)

6. **Be Gentle With Your Wellbeing**

We're going to take the safe bet that you don't need anything else to beat yourself up about. Improving and maintaining your wellbeing is a lifetime journey. While you can keep checking on your progress by using the PERMAH Workplace Survey to see what impact your efforts are having, your goal isn't to improve your score on a survey. The real score you want to see an improve around is your confidence be an intelligent and active steward of your wellbeing, so you have the knowledge, tools, and support you need to better navigate the highs and lows of work and life, and thrive more consistently.

Give yourself permission to try, to fail, to learn and to get up and try again. Be honest with yourself about where you are on the journey, be open to discovering better ways to care for yourself, and then use the PERMAH Workplace Survey and the interventions in this book—when you are ready—to take the next step. Know that you are worthy of feeling good and doing well.

Please remember that wellbeing is neither a one-shot, nor a one-size-fits-all affair. Different support tools work for different people at different times in their lives. If you believe you may benefit from extra support, we recommend using this book in conjunction with a trusted coach, psychologist, or doctor.

Just like you, when it comes to improving wellbeing, we're all learning. It's our hope that this book and the online tools we've provided help to make the journey a little faster, a little easier, and a lot more enjoyable for you.

Now, let's get started.

My Wellbeing Blueprint

1. **Measure Your Wellbeing:**

   Use the free online PERMAH Workplace Survey measure at www.permahsurvey.com.

2. **Reflect On Your Wellbeing:**

   What does your overall profile look like? Are there some areas that are higher or lower?

   ....

   ....

   How do you **feel** about your results? Are you surprised? Inspired? Disappointed?

   ....

   ....

   Are there any particular pillars drawing your attention? Why?

   ....

   ....

   ....

   Which areas are most important to you? How do you score on these pillars?

   ....

   ....

Are there any changes you'd like to create to help you feel better and do better over the coming months? Which PERMAH pillars does this suggest you should prioritize?

....

....

3. **Set Your Wellbeing Hopes:**

If you could invest your energy into **just** one or two of the PERMAH pillars right now, which ones would you most like improve?

....

What is the right time frame for you (for example, four, six, ten, or twelve weeks) to really see an improvement in your wellbeing?

....

Based on your life right now, what amount of daily time and energy is realistic for you to spend to improve your wellbeing? (For example, ten minutes, half an hour, an hour?)

....

4. **Choose Your Wellbeing Intervention:**

Once you've selected the PERMAH pillar or pillars you'd most like to improve and are clear on the time frame and time commitment you want to work within, turn to the chapter for that pillar and select a positive intervention you can't wait to get started on.

5. **Create Wellbeing Habits:**

   Can you create a small, busy-proof habit to embed this intervention into your day? What might be your:

   Cue: ....

   Routine: ....

   Reward: ....

6. **Be Gentle With Your Wellbeing:**

   Periodically, retake the PERMAH Workplace Survey to see what impact your efforts are having. What's working well with the interventions you're trying? What are you learning about how to improve your wellbeing? What impact do you feel your efforts are having? What do you want to try next?

   ....

   ....

   ....

   ....

   ....

   ....

   ....

   ....

   ....

   ....

CHAPTER 2

Promoting Positive Emotions

*"In the depth of winter, I finally learned that within me there
lay an invincible summer."* ~ Albert Camus, French philosopher

Researchers have found the experience of heartfelt positive emotions—like joy, gratitude, serenity, interest, hope, pride, amusement, inspiration, awe, and love—can help you to be more optimistic, resilient, open, accepting, and happier and healthier overall. When it comes to your work, they have also been found to improve your relationships, job satisfaction and success. But how?

Studies conducted by Professor Barbara Fredrickson from the University of North Carolina have repeatedly demonstrated that positive emotions help you to broaden and build the way your brain responds to opportunities and challenges. It turns out that positivity doesn't just change the content of your thinking, trading bad thoughts for good ones; it also changes the scope and boundaries of your mind, impacting your performance and wellbeing.

For example, positive emotions have been found to help you:

- See more of what's happening around you. Studies have found that when you are in a positive mood, your field of peripheral vision expands so you can take in about seventy-five percent of what's happening, compared to only fifteen percent in a neutral or negative mood.

- Think more quickly and creatively, by flooding your brain with the neurotransmitters dopamine and serotonin, which can help you make and sustain more neural connections. This helps you organize new information, do better on complex analysis and problem-solving tasks, and see and invent new ways of doing things.

- Connect and attune better to others. When your brain feels safe, you're more likely to think about "we" and less about "me." Studies have found that positivity broadens social responses by helping you feel closer to others, expanding your circle of trust, and overcoming bias.

While your experience of positive emotions may often feel brief and fleeting, it appears that just like putting money in the bank, as positive emotions accrue they help to build your psychological, social, intellectual, and physical resources, placing you on a positive trajectory of growth. This is because the broadened mindset that is enabled by the experience of positive emotions seems to be the basis for the discovery of new knowledge, new alliances, and new skills. In turn, these lead to more positive emotions, in what can be a positive spiral.

But, it is important to also remember that people who consistently thrive also experience negative emotions. In a world where rejection, failure, self-doubt, hypocrisy, loss, boredom, and annoying and obnoxious people are inevitable, you can't really be connected and grounded to life without encountering difficulties, challenges, and pain from time to time. While it can be tempting to ignore, suppress, or distract yourself from feelings of apprehension, anger, or sadness, these emotions can also offer important emotional, mental, and social learning opportunities.

For example, studies have found that:

- The right amount of anxiety can help you discover and shape solutions for risky situations or goals.

- A moderate degree of apprehension improves performance. An absence of anxiety results in apathy; too much can be paralyzing.

- Guilt can alert you to the hurt you have caused someone and motivate you to be more socially sensitive and caring.

- Anger can increase your optimism and creativity, and give you the energy to take action and do what counts.

- Sadness is a natural response to pain—in ourselves or others.

Rather than trying to avoid the discomfort these emotions can bring, researchers suggest your goal should be to feel robust enough to withstand emotional distress by being able to realize that these emotions are simply signs that something is not going right, to take the required actions, and to let the emotion pass. After all, emotions themselves are neither good nor bad; it's what you do with them that really matters.

That said, Fredrickson's research does suggest that it can be helpful to find the right balance between the frequency of heartfelt positive emotions and heart-straining negative emotions you experience each day. She suggests thinking of this like the balance of levity and gravity. Too much levity and you risk floating away and being disconnected from reality. But too many heart-straining negative emotions can put you at risk for being left flat on the floor, unable to get up. This can be the experience of a person with depression, who struggles to get out of bed. The negative emotions have overpowered the positive, leaving a sense of hopelessness and helplessness.

So what does the right balance of positive emotions look like? Because negative emotions have a stronger affect than positive emotions, researchers suggest that we need to experience more positive emotions each day than negative ones. Some researchers have suggested specific ratios, such as 3:1, 4:1, and 5:1. There is no magic ratio, and what is right depends on the person and the situation. But we can all benefit from infusing a bit more positivity into our own life and the lives of those around us.

Michelle's Story: A Practical Emotional Thermometer

Standing at my father's funeral, I thought that I might just drown in the waves of emotion I found myself swimming in. There was the expected sadness that a man's life had come to its end, and all the things he'd never have a chance to do. But there was also churning anger around the pain his alcoholism and abuse had inflicted on his family, relief that he couldn't hurt us anymore, and deep gratitude that this chapter in my life was finally done. All these emotions fought their way through my small five-foot frame as I stood there offering words of comfort to the family and friends who'd come to mourn him on that day.

As I drove home later, I remember thinking to myself: "Three months, Michelle. I'll give you three months to just surrender to the grief and get this over and done with. For three months it's okay to just function and find your way through all of this emotion." You see, when you study wellbeing for a living, one of the happy side effects is you end up experimenting with many of these ideas in your own life. As a result, up until my father's diagnosis of inoperable melanoma cancer three months earlier, I'd been consistently flourishing for some time.

But as you might expect, Dad's terminal diagnosis really put my wellbeing to the test. Not only was I suddenly responsible for making life and death decisions for a man I felt I hardly knew, but decades of trauma suddenly collided as my mostly estranged siblings were all thrown back together. The happy, stable, peaceful life I'd created was blown sky high as drug addiction, domestic abuse, sexual trauma, abandonment, and death all had to be confronted.

I longed to return to my previous state of flourishing, but I also knew that it was important to accept that in that moment—for all sorts of very good reasons—I was just functioning. And I knew it might stay that way for a while.

What I wanted to avoid during this incredibly challenging period was the risk of floundering. With a family history littered with depression, schizophrenia, bipolar disorder, and suicide, I didn't want my genes to take this opportunity to start expressing themselves in ways I'd managed to avoid so far. So I decided it would be worth a daily check-in on how I was navigating all of these emotions. Each evening, I completed the free two-minute survey at positivityratio.com.

It gave me a practical way to name, understand, and see the impact of the many emotions I was experiencing in the days after Dad's funeral. From the weeks filled with anger, to the months of sadness and the rays of hope and joy in between. In particular, I was trying to make sure my ratio didn't fall below 1:1. This was a good reminder that even on my lowest days, it was important to find small ways to bring heartfelt positivity into my experiences. Be it a walk on the beach, a cuddle with my kids, watching a silly cat video on YouTube, singing loudly and badly to an old favorite song, or time with good friends. I started to realize how these small moments were the key to finding the energy to heal.

Of course, three months after the funeral, when I looked again at where my positivity ratio lay, I realized it might take a little longer that I'd expected to really move back toward consistently flourishing. "Maybe we'll need three more months," I told myself.

Through this period, I continued to monitor and be mindful of the balance of heartfelt positivity and heart-straining negativity flowing through my days. And I started to find that as I adapted to the new world I found myself in and anger began to fade, I began to have more energy to invest in activities of heartfelt positivity, like using my strengths to create exciting new projects at work, to reengaging in daily meditative practice and regular yoga classes.

When this next three months had passed and I looked at my ratio, I could see that while I was making steady progress, I still wasn't flourishing the way I had in the past. So I took a deep breath and gave myself another three months.

Nine months after my Dad passed, I finally felt like I had emerged from the fog of grief and was consistently flourishing once more as I navigated my way through the world. At a time when I felt unable to deal with more than the most basic details of life, taking my daily emotional temperature had felt like a manageable way to ensure that if I was starting to flounder I could catch it early and get the support I needed in those moments. It also gave me small, practical ways to slowly move myself back toward flourishing.

Peggy's Story: Embracing Emotion

I was skeptical of the field of positive psychology from the beginning. The idea of a science focused on making people happy seemed like an idea dreamed up by overenthusiastic optimists. I had experienced enough of life by that point to know that it can be hard work.

When I was a graduate student at the University of California, Riverside, I was part of the Mortality Lab—we looked at what made people at risk of illness and early mortality, versus those who live long, healthy lives. My roommates were part of the Happiness Lab. Interestingly, the two labs studied some of the same things—many of the predictors of happiness also predict good health and longevity. The mind and body are closely connected and my first academic paper was an intersection of the two. With Professor Sonja Lyubomirsky and Dr. Ryan Howell, we conducted a large review of studies that looked at the effects of positive affect on health outcomes.

I went on to a postdoc position at the Positive Psychology Center at the University of Pennsylvania—the hub of American positive psychology— where I worked under the supervision of Professors Martin Seligman and Angela Duckworth. I taught in the Masters of Applied Positive Psychology program, and did numerous studies focused on understanding, measuring, and building wellbeing. While I remained skeptical, I came to better understand and appreciate the positive psychology perspective. Claims coming from popular articles and books can teeter on the edge of unsubstantiated self-help, but there's also a lot of good scholarship going on. While there is a big focus on positive emotion, it's really about recognizing the entire mental health spectrum, and how one's mental health ebbs and flows across the situations, contexts, and experiences of life.

And so I found myself moving across the world to Melbourne, Australia, with a job title of "Senior Lecturer in Positive Psychology." I guess that makes me a positive psychologist, although I think I'm more of a negative psychologist who studies wellbeing. I have struggled with mental health issues for years. I'll have periods where I'm doing well and enjoying life. There are other times when I find life really difficult. But I also have an entire toolset at my fingertips, helping me to take control of my mental health. As much as I once would have hated to admit it, many of the positive psychology exercises for building wellbeing really do help.

I have several positive exercises that I often draw on to support my wellbeing. It's the little things that matter. Staying physically active and spending time in nature are particularly useful. Then there are the little pick-me-ups during the day—a cup of hot coffee, a walk around the block, a piece of chocolate, a warm shower, a pretty picture. I also benefit from focusing on gratitude. In times of struggle, it's easy to become critical and bitter. By purposely noticing the good things around me, it cuts through the negative emotions, stopping what can become a negative spiral.

I love the Pixar movie *Inside Out*. At first glance, it captures the stereotypical image of positive psychology—everything is about joy. Just be happy and everything will work out. But as the movie unfolds, joy ultimately breaks down. It's by embracing all the emotions that true wellbeing emerges. By taking control of my mental health through little, everyday positive behaviors, it doesn't mean I'll bounce off the walls with exuberant excitement, but it does mean that I can feel calmer and more at peace with life, despite the challenges I might be facing. And maybe that's what true joy is.

Cultivating *Positive* Emotions

DIALING UP POSITIVITY	Jolts of Joy
DIALING DOWN NEGATIVITY	Create Healthy Distractions
PRACTICING KINDNESS	Track Your Kindness
CULTIVATING GRATITUDE	Count Your Blessings
SAVORING THE GOOD	Immerse Yourself
GETTING COMFORTABLY UNCOMFORTABLE	Name Your Emotions
SHORT-CIRCUITING STRESS	Decode Stress Messages

Hunt & Gather	Connect With Nature	Measure Your Positivity
Disrupt Negative Thoughts	Navigate Negativity Landmines	Limit Media Time
Have A Kindness Day	Try Loving Kindness Meditation	Random Acts of Kindness
Write A Gratitude Letter	Carry A Gratitude Scrap	Thank One Person
Re-Live Peak Moments	Savor Your Stories	What Went Well
Slow Down Your Responses	Control The Controllables	Get Into Your Body
Turn Adversity Into A Resource	Set Stretch Goals	Re-Frame Stress Moments

Dialing Up Positivity

Can you find ways to bring more positive emotion into your day? Experiencing heartfelt positive emotion creates an upward spiral of wellbeing that can broaden and build your psychological resources, allowing you to be more open to possibilities, connect with others, and build your resilience and wellbeing. While negative emotions like anxiety, stress, and anger are also a part of life, too many can create a downward spiral that narrows your thinking, making it harder to see the bigger picture or to ask for help when you need it. Finding ways to prevent the bad from eclipsing the good can help you maintain your wellbeing, despite your circumstances.

How can I develop more heartfelt positivity?

You can't create genuine heartfelt positive emotion by just trying to think happy thoughts. Willpower and mental effort alone are not enough to make a difference. Instead, studies suggest that the most reliable and effective way to alter your emotional state is to try and better select or modify your circumstances. For example, if you enjoy having dinner parties with friends, this can be a great way to set the stage for more heartfelt positivity. But, hosting a dinner party can be a lot of work, so as the experience unfolds you may need to modify the situation in small ways. For instance, you could spend more time interacting with your guests rather than being in the kitchen—see how this impacts what you're feeling. It's also important to be realistic about your expectations of positivity. Positive emotions are fleeting. They're going to arise and they're going to dissipate, and we need to accept that, rather than try to cling to them.

What can I try?

- **Jolts Of Joy:** Write down five jolts of joy—something that genuinely brings a smile to your face—that you can quickly reach for when you need to inject some heartfelt positivity. It might be a favorite song, a funny YouTube clip, poetry you love, cartoons you enjoy, someone who always makes you laugh, a place that brings you peace, or a game that relaxes you. Keep your jolts of joy list somewhere handy—on your desk, on your phone, or in the front page of your diary. When you feel negativity narrowing in, reach for a jolt of joy, and notice how your brain responds.

- **Hunt And Gather:** Create a portfolio of positivity by collecting letters, photos, quotes, or objects that have a deep personal meaning for you and elicit positive emotion. Start with gratitude, and then move to joy, serenity, curiosity, hope, pride, amusement, inspiration, awe, and love. Slowly build one portfolio at a time and give yourself the space to appreciate each item. Then, let your portfolios be living collections by adding to them when you can. When you need a positivity boost, bring out a portfolio, and really savor the positive emotions associated with each memento. Engage with it mindfully and let your heart open to the positive emotions that arise.

- **Connect With Nature:** Get out regularly into nature and spend time enjoying the eternal beauty and presence of the world around you. It might be sitting under a tree, walking through a park or along a river, or stopping to take in a sunset. Allow yourself to drink in the wonder, majesty, and timelessness of the natural world.

Is there a habit I can play with?

Before you brush your teeth each night (cue), take the free two-minute survey at **http://www.positivityratio.com** to **Measure Your Positivity**. Make a note of what's creating heartfelt positivity for you and how you might build upon this tomorrow. Also note what's creating heart-straining negativity and how you can manage this better tomorrow (routine). Then, brush your teeth (reward) and head to bed.

Dialing Down Negativity

Do you find yourself getting stuck in thoughts about all the things going wrong in your life or the world? Perhaps it's a mistake you made at work, a colleague who's being difficult, or world events that leave you feeling completely overwhelmed. Studies suggest that while ruminating like this might feel like a way of working things out, it can quickly spin out of control and zap your energy, diminish your confidence, and reduce engagement with life. Finding ways to break this cycle of overthinking can make a huge difference to your wellbeing. The good news is that it only takes a few minutes to break the trajectory of a downward spiral, but the benefits of the turnaround are long-lasting and transformational.

How can I develop less recycled negativity?

Once you've learned from a negative experience, it's important not to let what's unfolded continue to weigh you down. Try not to prolong bad feelings beyond the insight and growth they have provided, by noticing what triggers these patterns of obsessive thinking. For example, being constantly tuned into the news media may be derailing your focus and fueling your negative emotions, so it may be helpful to limit how often you monitor the news. Being mindful about how often and with whom you share your negative feelings could help you avoid re-triggering vulnerabilities in yourself and others. Instead of ruminating over what's worrying you, let yourself be distracted with a good novel, hunt for good news stories, or get out into the world.

What can I try?

- **Create Healthy Distractions:** Divide a page into two columns. In the first column, write the heading "Healthy Distractions" and list as many easily-done, highly-engaging activities you can think of. You might include playing an instrument, doing some gardening, watching a new TED talk, playing with your child, or practicing meditative breathing.

In the second column, write the heading "Unhealthy Distractions" and list all the things you typically do to take your mind off things that might not be serving you well—for example, reaching for a piece of chocolate, buying things you don't need, or gossiping about other people. Make sure you have at least one healthy alternative distraction for each unhealthy distraction you identify. You can add to the list over time as you notice the activities you switch to when stress or overthinking kicks in. Keep your list handy so you're prepared to distract yourself with a healthy activity whenever rumination starts.

- **Disrupt Negative Thoughts:** Grab a set of index cards and write down your negative thoughts, such as: "I'm such an idiot. I'm always messing things up." Try to write down exactly what you say to yourself. Do this for a few days; you'll probably be shocked at just how frequently negative self-talk occurs. Then, shuffle the cards and pick one at random. Read it out loud. Then—as fast and as thoroughly as you can—dispute it! Do it out loud and with conviction. Is this belief really true? Are you one hundred percent sure? In what ways is it not true? Could there be any other plausible explanation? Which explanation will serve you best in this situation? When you're satisfied that your rapid-fire facts have shot down your menacing negativity, tear up the card, and throw it away. Keep adding to your cards whenever you find negativity lurking in your mind. You can also take a playful approach by singing or reading your card aloud in an exaggerated accent or a silly voice (try Mickey Mouse or Arnold Schwarzenegger). This technique will often change a painful criticism into something hilariously absurd and lessen its power over you.

- **Navigate Negativity Landmines:** Reflect on your typical daily routine at work and ask yourself: "Which activities or events trigger the most negativity for me?" Is it your commute? Particular meetings? Interactions with certain colleagues or clients? Once you've rounded up your emotional landmines, ask yourself: "Is this negativity necessary? Is it helpful?" Can you avoid or modify the situation to feel more positive about it? Can you be better prepared for it or change what it means or causes you to think? Could this be an unexpected learning opportunity? Play with these approaches each time a negativity landmine explodes until you feel calmer and more confident in navigating these moments.

- **Limit Media Time:** Unfortunately, most of the media coverage you watch, listen to, or read contains more bad news than good news, which can overload you with negative emotions. Be mindful of how the media you're consuming is making you feel. If it's creating unnecessary heart-straining negativity, find more positive ways to stay attuned to what's happening in the world. If you want to mix in more positivity, visit sites such as Upworthy and the Good News Network.

Is there a habit I can play with?

Set aside fifteen minutes during the day as your "Worry Time" (cue). Outside this time, acknowledge your worrying thoughts, but don't focus on them. Instead, refocus your attention on the matter at hand. Aim to schedule your worry time when you tend to be the most relaxed—for example, after exercise or doing something you enjoy—and stick to the time limit you have set (routine). At the end of your worry time, reward yourself with a favorite drink (reward) and feel it washing or dissolving all your worries away.

Practicing Kindness

How does doing a kind act for someone make you feel? Studies suggest that kind people experience more happiness and gratitude and have more positive memories, because acts of kindness help to highlight your abilities, your resources, and your expertise and give you a sense of confidence, optimism, usefulness, and meaning. What's more, the positive emotions you derive from giving to others have been found to create a positive feedback loop because kindness is contagious—people who witness your kind act are more likely to be kind as well.

How can I develop more kindness?

Researchers argue that kindness is like a muscle that needs to be strengthened through repeated use. For example, it seems that kind behavior comes more naturally when you're feeling a sense of compassion and connection with others, regularly making the choice to give to others (yes, even on days when you're not in a particularly generous mood), and finding ways to inspire others toward kindness. For more ideas and inspiration visit the Random Acts of Kindness website: **www.randomactsofkindness.org**.

What can I try?

- **Track Your Kindness:** Keep a journal and write down the acts of kindness you give and receive. These acts might vary in size—offer someone a genuine compliment; volunteer to do an unpopular household chore; let someone else go first in the coffee queue; donate money to a charity; or take time to really listen to someone. The goal is to increase your awareness of the good you're doing and receiving in everyday life.

- **Have A Kindness Day:** Choose one day of the week and make this your kindness day. On this day, set yourself the challenge of doing five kind things for others. It could be holding the door open for someone, helping someone with directions, thanking a friend or colleague, or buying a pay-it-forward coffee. Notice how this leaves you feeling.

- **Try Loving-Kindness Meditation:** This is a powerful way to send goodwill, kindness, and warmth to others by silently repeating a series of mantras. Loving-kindness meditation involves mentally visualizing four steps: receiving loving-kindness, sending it to a person close to you, sending it to neutral people, and then sending it to all of humankind. Find a guided meditation to suit you at **www.positivityresonance.com/ meditations.**

Is there a habit I can play with?

When you turn on your computer each morning (cue), take five minutes to perform a **Random Act Of Kindness** for a colleague or client (routine). For example, you could connect people in your network who can help each other; email an idea or a piece of research; send a note of thanks; or give some positive feedback about someone to their boss. And only when it's done, grab your morning cup of coffee or tea (reward).

Cultivating Gratitude

How grateful do you feel for the good things in your life? Gratitude is much more than being glad for a gift or kind act, it's also experiencing a sense of wonder, thankfulness, and appreciation for life. It involves noticing and appreciating the good things in and around you. Consistently feeling grateful for the good things in your life and what makes them possible has been found to improve your relationships, boost your levels of energy and positivity, head off adaptation (when you become desensitized through familiarity), and deal with negative emotions and adversity. Studies suggest that people who are regularly grateful are generally more optimistic, successful, healthier, and happier. In fact, gratitude is regarded by some researchers as a "mega-strategy" for achieving happiness.

How can I develop more gratitude?

Research has found that gratitude has two parts. Firstly, it's an affirmation of the good things in your life, the world around you, and for the gifts and benefits you've received. This doesn't mean ignoring that there are challenges, hassles, and sadness in life, but it does help you to intentionally look for the good things and bring more balance to your thoughts and feelings. Secondly, it's about recognizing the external sources of good. It's humbly acknowledging that others help you in big or small ways. Studies suggest that one of the best ways to cultivate more gratitude is to have a daily practice of intentionally noticing and appreciating what's working well in your life and why.

What can I try?

- **Count Your Blessings:** Once a week, take a few moments to write down five things that happened that week for which you are grateful. The five things need not be of earth-shattering importance, but they do need to matter to you. Note what made each of these things possible. For example, if you were grateful for a rare team lunch, you could note:

"Catching up with the team. Possible because I made the time in my calendar." Research indicates that once a week is ideal for this activity, as studies show that many people become bored of the practice if done too frequently.

- **Write A Gratitude Letter:** Think of a person you've never had the chance to meaningfully thank—they might be a relative, friend, colleague, or even a teacher or writer who influenced you. Given the opportunity, what would you thank them for, and why? Take the time to write a letter to this person, expressing your appreciation for the positive impact they've had on your life. If you'd like, deliver your letter to the person and read it aloud to them, or simply give it to them with heartfelt thanks. Don't worry if it's not possible to give the person the letter, the process of writing the letter itself can be enough to boost your wellbeing.

- **Carry A Gratitude Scrap:** Each morning before you leave for work, spend a few minutes writing down three things you're grateful for and carry that scrap of paper all day long, glancing at it when you need some positivity in your day.

Is there a habit I can play with?

At the end of each work day (cue), take the time to genuinely **Thank One Person** for how they made your day a little better or a little easier. Do it face-to-face if you can, but if not, a call, SMS, or email is fine. Be specific about what you appreciated and why (routine). Then head home (reward).

Savoring The Good

How often do you take the time to relish the good things in your life? Savoring is the act of mindfully trying to prolong and/or intensify an emotion or experience. It's the idea that you should "stop and smell the roses." By intentionally enjoying the good things in your life for as long as possible, studies have found you can boost your feelings of joy, hope, optimism, love, contentment, and gratitude, while creating an upward spiral of happiness that enhances your feelings of wellbeing, strengthens your relationships, and increases your resilience in difficult times.

How can I develop more savoring?

Savoring involves magnifying and extending positive experiences by paying attention to and appreciating them. This can be as they occur in the present moment, a reminiscence about the past, or in anticipation of a planned event for the future (such as a holiday or special celebration). Your goal is to take something that is already good and transform it into something even better by becoming fully immersed in the experience. Researchers suggest you can extend the benefits of these emotions by sharing the story with someone you are close to, journaling about the experience, or taking a photograph or keeping a memento to remind you of the experience.

What can I try?

- **Immerse Yourself:** Each day, try to catch yourself during one pleasant experience and immerse all your senses in what's unfolding. Take a mental picture of what's unfolding in this moment. For example, if it's a home-cooked meal, you might notice the fragrant aromas, the warmth and flavor of the food in your mouth, or the good company of the people sharing the meal with you.

- **Relive Peak Moments:** For three days, spend fifteen minutes writing about a treasured or exciting memory. On the second and third day, you can either write about the same experience or choose a different one. Recall a wonderful experience or one of your happiest moments—perhaps it was a moment of awe, being in love, spending time with people important to you, or experiencing an "aha moment" from a book, talk, or artwork. Try to fully relive the experience, including all the associated feelings and emotions. Then, write as much detail as you can, noting everything that happened, how you felt, what you were thinking, other people's reactions, and why this experience is meaningful to you.

- **Savor Your Stories:** At least twice a week, share a story of something good that you've experienced with someone who is important to you. Try to relive the positive emotion as you retell the story. Encourage that person to share a story with you. Enjoy the positive emotions that arise.

Is there a habit I can play with?

During your evening meal (cue), share a story around the table about the best part of your day or **What Went Well**. It could be a funny story, someone who inspired you, something you did and feel really proud of, or a plan that you've made and are looking forward to (routine). Notice and savor the positive emotions that come with this moment (reward).

Getting Comfortably Uncomfortable

How do you handle feelings of anxiety, fear, anger, sadness, guilt, shame, distrust, or hate? While it can be tempting to suppress or distract yourself from these feelings, researchers have found that developing distress tolerance—being able to shift to the upside or the downside of your emotions to get the best possible outcome for the situation—can help you to become a better learner, be more successful, and experience the deepest sense of wellbeing in life.

How can I develop distress tolerance?

Rather than dismissing or trying to avoid your negative emotions, try using them as helpful signals that something important to you isn't right and needs your attention. Studies suggest that you can build your confidence for distress tolerance by learning to name how you're feeling, understanding why these emotions are occurring and what they are trying to guide you toward, and then choosing how much attention you give them so you can withstand the pain these emotions can bring. You may find it also helps to remind yourself that all emotions are transient by nature, and will come and go.

What can I try?

- **Name Your Emotions:** When you experience emotional discomfort, take a few moments to tune in and notice what's happening in your body. Breathe in slowly and sit with how you're feeling. Then try to identify the negative emotions you are experiencing. You may even want to say to yourself: "Hello worry," if that's what you're feeling. Recognizing and naming the emotion can help you shift to being an observer of the painful emotion. Understand that while you are experiencing worry right now, this does not mean you are a "worrier"; the experience will pass.

- **Slow Down Your Responses:** When you experience a strong emotion such as anger, slow down your response so you can respectfully and appropriately respond in ways that will be most helpful for the situation. Take a few deep breaths. Then visualize your anger as a car speedometer. If you think your anger is too high in response to the situation, then take a few moments to breathe deeply to put the brakes on and slow down your reaction. Continue to check your emotional reaction speed during the interaction.

- **Control The Controllables:** Reflect on a challenging situation that's consistently causing you to experience some negative emotions. Make a list of what you can control and then identify the actions on which you want to focus your attention, energy and efforts.

Is there a habit I can play with?

Get Into Your Body. On your way to work each morning (cue), tune into how your body is feeling and notice if there are any negative emotions you're holding on to. Are your shoulders hunched? Is your jaw tight? Is your stomach swirling? Are you feeling agitated? If you find you're not feeling great, try to name the emotions you're experiencing and tune into what might be causing them. What are they trying to tell you? Is there any action you need to take? Do you need to remind yourself that this feeling will pass and focus your attention on the things you can control? (routine). Then buy yourself a morning coffee, tea, or snack to get your day started (reward).

Short-Circuiting Stress

Have you ever wished your life was less stressful? With media headlines like, "Stress Kills" or "Science Proves Stress Makes You Depressed," it's easy to understand why most of us become pretty anxious when we're feeling stressed. Research makes a distinction between a stressor (something that challenges us) and stress (the perception that you are unable to cope with the stressor). We often confuse the two, which leads to the idea that all stress is bad. But studies find that there can also be benefits to stress. For example, stress can increase the risk of health problems—except when people regularly see a benefit in their struggles. Stress can be debilitating—except when it helps you perform. Indeed, a total lack of stress results in underperformance.

You see, stress itself appears to be neither good nor bad. We are constantly facing internal and external stresses, and the body is amazingly resilient to those stresses. While your genes and life history can influence your stress response, it seems that it is your beliefs about stress that most shape the actions you're willing to take and the outcomes you're most likely to get.

How can I develop better stress responses?

Researchers suggest seeing the good in stress doesn't require abandoning the awareness that, in some cases, stress is harmful. Rather, what matters is the ability to notice the opportunities for learning, growth, and connection as you try to cope with things that are difficult and challenging. The mindset shift allows you to hold a more balanced view of stress—to fear it less, to trust yourself to handle it, and to use it as a resource for engaging with life. Instead of an exercise in positive thinking, think of it as an exercise in being able to hold opposite or competing perspectives simultaneously—the ability to see the "and" rather than the "either/or."

What can I try?

- **Decode Stress Messages:** Acknowledge when you are feeling stressed and welcome it as your body's way of telling you something that matters to you is at risk. Can you connect to the positive motivation behind the stress? What is at stake here, and why does it matter to you? Which part of the stress response do you need most right now? Do you need to fight, escape, engage, connect, find meaning, or grow? Even if it feels like your stress response is pushing you in one direction, focusing on how you want to respond can shift your biology to support you. If there is a stress response you would like to develop, consider what it would look like in any stressful situation you are dealing with now. Try to make use of the energy stress gives you, instead of wasting that energy trying to manage your stress. What can you do right now that reflects your values and your goals? What strengths can you draw on to respond in the way you want?

- **Turn Adversity Into A Resource:** Call to mind a stressful situation where you persevered or learned something. Take a few moments to consider what this taught you about your strengths or how you cope with adversity. For fifteen minutes, write about the experience. Use these questions to guide your writing:

  - What did you do that helped you get through it?

  - What personal resources and personal strengths did you draw on?

  - Did you seek advice or support?

  - What did this teach you about dealing with adversity?

  - How did this experience make you stronger?

  - How can you apply this learning to future challenges?

- **Set Stretch Goals:** Eleanor Roosevelt suggested doing one thing every day that scares you. Researchers agree that setting stretch goals that are difficult and meaningful can give you plenty of practice at fine-tuning your stress responses. As you take on these goals, commit to having open and honest conversations with yourself about how you're managing your stress, what you're learning from your mistakes, and how you can show up in similar experiences in the future so you can access your brain's neurological wiring for hope.

Is there a habit I can play with?

Reframe Stress Moments. When you plan your day (cue), place a star next to the most stressful task on your list and write a note about the stress response (fight-and-flight, challenge-and-grow, or tend-and-befriend) you'd like to harness for this situation so that your brain is primed for the experience (routine). As you wrap up the task or cross it off your list, give yourself a score out of ten (reward) for how well you navigated the stress you experienced and note what you can try during tomorrow's stressful task.

CHAPTER 3

Enhancing Engagement

"We work not only to produce, but to give value to time."
~ Eugene Delacroix, French artist

Engagement has become a catch phrase in organizations, with many people feeling disengaged at work. Employers are concerned about "presenteeism"— being physically there, but mentally elsewhere. For some, work is boring. For others, there are simply too many distractions. Attention wanders, tasks seem uninteresting, and energy wanes.

Engagement is the feeling you get when you're fully absorbed in what you're doing. It's that feeling of "being in the zone" or "one with the music" that comes when time seems to stop, and you lose all sense of consciousness. Performing at your best feels absolutely effortless and you're left feeling genuinely proud of what you've been able to accomplish.

Professor Mihaly Csikszentmihalyi, of Claremont Graduate University, describes a state of high engagement as "flow." Researchers suggest that experiencing a state of flow comes with a host of benefits. In these moments, you feel more involved in your life, rather than isolated from it. You enjoy activities far more, rather than feeling bored. You have a stronger sense of control, rather than feelings of helplessness that can overwhelm you. You also enjoy a stronger sense of self, have more self-belief, and a higher level of confidence in what you're actually capable of doing.

Csikszentmihalyi has found that flow is more likely to occur when you have a clear goal that balances your skill level with the complexity of the task at hand; when you feel a sense of autonomy and choice about how you're approaching the task; and when you receive regular feedback on how you're doing. In flow, your skills are fully utilized, stretched to a manageable limit so you're learning, growing, improving, and advancing.

Flow is more likely to occur if you create internal and external conditions that help focus your interests and attention on the task at hand. Internally, it's easier to stay engaged when a task is personally interesting and meaningful. This means there is benefit in getting to know yourself—what you like doing and what you are good at—and then apply these strengths to the tasks you take on. Externally, there are a lot of distractions in our everyday lives. Think about how you can create distraction-free time and space throughout your day. It's all about working smarter, not harder.

Figuring out what your strengths are—those things you are good at and actually enjoy doing—is often one of the first steps toward creating more moments of flow. But the key to consistently feeling engaged in what you're doing isn't simply to use your strengths more—this can be the path to all sorts of unintended negative outcomes. Rather, it is figuring out how to use the right strength, in the right amount, for the right outcomes.

You see, when you're feeling bored, lacking confidence, or finding yourself procrastinating and putting things off, chances are you're underplaying the strengths that would serve you best for the task you're delaying. There will also be times when you feel like your strengths are perfectly matched to a task, but things aren't quite going according to plan; people might be complaining about your work or you may feel on the verge of burning out. These are signs that you're probably overplaying your strengths in this situation. In fact, we've found that if you scratch the surface of most of the "weaknesses" or "improvement" feedback you've ever been given, you'll find that it's a strength being overplayed.

And of course, being strengths-focused doesn't mean you have to ignore your weaknesses. It just means you understand that when it comes to creating more moments of engagement, developing your strengths allows you to work with the ways your brain is already wired to perform at its best, and thus more readily access the state of flow. Some researchers suggest that applying an eighty percent focus on developing your strengths and a twenty percent focus on fixing your weaknesses at work may be a good way to balance your efforts.

It's also necessary to create conditions that allow engagement to occur. Distractions make it hard to stay engaged. You sit down to work on a project, and emails pop up, people stop by to chat, and you are pulled into yet another meeting. Technology constantly pulls on your attention, making it a challenge to focus on the task at hand, despite your best intentions. Finding ways to structure your schedule and environment to reduce distractions can help you engage and be more productive.

Michelle's Story: Finding Flow In Any Job

When I first discovered my strengths, I was working in New York as the global brand director for one of the world's largest firms. I thought it was going to be my dream job, so you can imagine my dismay when six months into the role I found myself absolutely dreading the idea of going to work. On paper everything looked great, but in reality the job was sucking all the energy and joy from me. And I couldn't figure out what I was doing wrong.

It was around this time I completed my first strengths assessment tool and discovered that one of my top strengths was Curiosity. I realized that I was struggling to find ways to use this strength in my new job. I'd reached a level of technical mastery in branding that meant there weren't many new challenges, and as a result I was completely underplaying my strength of curiosity at work. It was a career changing—and eventually, life changing—aha moment.

Starting the very next day, I decided that when I first got to work each morning, I'd spend at least ten minutes reading and learning something new that I could apply to my work. I started with every book or article I could lay my hands on about understanding my strengths and over time expanded this to the fields of Positive Psychology and Wellbeing. I could have spent all day learning about how to bring out the best in myself and others, so I had to set my alarm to remind me to stop after ten minutes. And then I'd reward myself by—and I understand this is a little sad—opening my emails. (What can I tell you? It's like an itch I have to scratch each morning!)

It took less than a week before this tiny, daily strengths habit had me looking forward to getting into the office. Within a month, I felt reengaged, energized, and happy about my job. And to my boss' delight, my performance—and eventually that of my team as I taught them how to develop their strengths as well—skyrocketed on every objective measure. In fact, nine months later, my boss suggested that in order to really put my strengths to work, perhaps I should start teaching these ideas to others in the company. And the rest, as they say, is history.

Peggy's Story: Lost In The Moment

The flight attendant's voice cuts through my reverie, pulling my eyes from the computer screen. "Dr. Kern, here is your special meal." The countdown ticker on the airplane map shows two hours to go on the flight back to Melbourne. Where did the time go? I write a bit more as I eat, thoughts and ideas swirling in my mind, coalescing into the words of the article. As the other passengers wake up and start moving about, my attention is broken. I give up trying to work, knowing my focus is gone. The rest of the time drags by until we finally touch down.

Over the past few years, I've done a lot of traveling. As an American living in Australia, it's a long way home. I've had opportunities to give talks, meet with people, and teach across the United States, Australia, Japan, China,

Iran, Colombia, France, and Scotland, to name just a few of the countries I've visited. With some of these flights requiring more than thirty hours of travel each way, I've spent a lot of hours sitting on planes.

While most people dread being cooped up for what can feel like endless hours on an international flight, I've learned that the best way to make the time to pass is to find ways to become more engaged in what I'm doing. This might include catching up on movies, meeting strange and interesting people, or mentally taking a pause from the craziness of life.

Increasingly, I've also come to pass the hours on planes by writing. As an academic, my career depends on publishing articles and book chapters, and each one takes a considerable amount of effort as I'm pushed to the edges of my intellectual abilities. It's like solving a complex puzzle that requires all of my attention, as I try to find the best way to make sense of the data and tell a meaningful story.

Unfortunately, when I'm on the ground, between emails, telephone calls, meetings, and more, my attention is constantly being pulled in different directions. As I feel the deadlines ticking closer and I struggle to find the space I need to focus, my mind starts to freeze, my stress levels increase, and anxiety starts to consume me. Articles can sit untouched for weeks or months on end. I let people down. I feel like I'm barely functioning.

But on the plane, for twelve to eighteen hours, no one can reach me. I can become immersed in the data, and the stories within it seem to emerge as if by magic. Writing becomes pleasurable and, as I lose myself in the moment, the hours fly by. It has become one of my most engaging and productive times. And as I feel myself making progress toward the commitments I value, my sense of balance is restored and I land feeling alive once more.

Creating Opportunities For Engagement Toolkit

Discover Your Strengths	Name Your Strengths	See Your Reflected Best Self	Have A Daily Strengths Reflection	Use Your Strengths Each Day
Creating Moments Of Flow	Meet Your Best Possible Self	Craft Your Job	Create A ROAD MAP	Finding Moments Of Flow
Developing Your Strengths	Use Your Strengths In A New Way	Take A Mindful Strengths Pause	Invest In A Daily Strengths Habit	
Being Mindful	Eat Mindfully	Look For What's Novel	Embrace Not Knowing	Meditate Daily
Staying Playful	Create Your Play History	Be Playful	Get Active	Try Rapid Prototyping

Discovering Your Strengths

Do you have the chance to do what you do best each day? Studies find that when you have the opportunity to use your strengths (those things you are good at and actually enjoy doing), you are likely to feel more confident, creative, engaged, and satisfied with your work and your life. You see, a strength represents the way your brain is wired to perform at its best. Over time you've practiced these particular thoughts, feelings, and behaviors so often that you've built up neural pathways that make it easier, more effective, and more enjoyable to work in these ways.

How can I discover my strengths?

Researchers suggest the first step is to become aware of what your strengths are by completing a strengths assessment tool or gathering reflections from yourself and others about your best moments and identifying the strengths you're drawing on. Then, you'll need to explore your past and current experiences and how these strengths serve you well or can be underplayed or overplayed in different situations. Finally, you'll want to find ways to apply your strengths more consistently in daily life.

What can I try?

- **Name Your Strengths:** Use one of the online strengths assessment tools to help you identify your strengths. Gallup Strengths Finder (gallupstrengthscenter.com) and the Strengths Profile (strengthsprofile. com) are paid assessments you can use. Or, we like the free, ten-minute VIA Survey (viacharacter.org). These tools will give you an easy way to start exploring and applying your strengths more consistently. The websites also provide a lot of information about the strengths, including details on what they are and strategies for applying them in your day-to-day life.

- **See Your Reflected Best Self:** Ask at least five people from different contexts in your life to write down a story about a time when they've seen you really engaged, energized, and enjoying what you were doing. What was happening in this moment? Why is it so memorable for them? Which strengths did they see you using? As you review these stories, look for common themes of how your strengths showed up in your best moments. (If you'd like to purchase a kit to guide you through these steps visit: (michellemcquaid.com/reflected-best-self-exercise/).

- **Have A Daily Strengths Reflection:** At the end of each day, take a few minutes to journal about what you discovered about your strengths today. Did you experience moments of flow? If yes, which strengths were you drawing on and how can you keep building on these tomorrow? Did you underplay or overplay any of your strengths? If yes, how can you dial these strengths up or down tomorrow?

Is there a habit I can play with?

Each week, pick one of your strengths to explore more fully. Then, when you first wake up (cue), read, reflect, or look for ways this strength is used by yourself or others. Think about how it is used effectively, underplayed, or overplayed by people. Look for ways you could apply it that day (routine). Then hit the shower (reward). This way, you will **Use Your Strenths Each Day.**

Creating Moments Of Flow

What might be possible if you used your strengths in a state of flow every single day? While this might sound like an impossible dream, creating the space to vividly visualize positive images of your future can fuel you with hope and put you on the road to finding solutions, helping you to realize that you have the power to make things happen. Studies suggest that imagining what is possible triggers your brain's neural reward system, kick-starting a cascade of dopamine through key pathways, and helping you move from intention to action and boosting your levels of optimism, motivation, and feelings of control.

How can I create more opportunities for flow?

Researchers suggest that while your strengths exist within you and are a reflection of how your brain is wired to perform at its best, they are also shaped by the situations in which you are immersed. By getting clear on which strengths you'd most like to develop and ways you can effectively draw on them, studies have found this can build understanding of your motives, help restructure your priorities, and enhance your self-regulation abilities and sense of control.

What can I try?

- **Meet Your Best Possible Self:** Once you're clear on what your strengths are, grab a piece of paper and spend fifteen to twenty minutes journaling in a stream of consciousness about what might be possible in the year ahead if you were using your strengths regularly each day in a state of flow and everything went as well as it possibly could. Try to capture as vividly as possible what you'd be doing each day and which strengths you'd be drawing upon, what others would notice and value about your efforts, and why you'd feel truly proud of what you were able to achieve. Don't overthink it. Don't edit it. Just let it pour out. If you can, repeat this exercise for three days in a row before reviewing what you've written, noting which ideas that are charged with the most energy and those that fill you with hope. Think about how you can start making these a reality.

- **Craft Your Job:** Write down all the tasks required in your job, then divide them into those you enjoy and those you feel drained by. Now, think about what you could do to increase the things you enjoy doing. This might involve changing the type and number of tasks you undertake, thinking about who you spend your time with or how you perceive pillars of your work, or reframe how you think about a task. Then experiment with what's possible. Move past your own expectations of how you "should" spend your time and find small moments—even if it's at lunchtime or just before your day starts—to use your strengths and feel more fully engaged each day.

- **Create A ROAD MAP:** Fuse your strengths with the practice of mindfulness using the ROAD MAP technique:

  - **Reflect:** Take time out to think about ways you have used your strengths in your past successes and struggles.

  - **Observe:** Rather than trying to spot a particular strength, simply observe your environment and the people around you with curiosity and interest. Which strengths pop up?

  - **Appreciate:** Tell others about how you value their strengths. Name the strengths you see in them and share with them where and how you saw them display these strengths.

  - **Discuss:** Communicate with others about your strengths. Allow "strengths of character" to be your topic of conversation.

  - **Monitor:** In a log or journal, track your strengths by writing down your use of your signature strengths, lower strengths, or particular strengths you want to enhance.

  - **Ask:** Get feedback from your family, friends, coworkers, and neighbors on the strengths you use. What strengths do others see that you don't see?

- **Plan:** Set a goal around a strength you'd like to display more often. Write down ways you can use this strength in your everyday routine so that it can be integrated into the things you do each day.

Is there a habit I can play with?

When you're planning your week (cue), take a few minutes to write down what might be possible this week if you were able to regularly use your strengths in a state of flow and everything went as well as possible (routine). What would you prioritize? How would you use your strengths to approach different tasks? What would others value about your efforts? Why would you feel proud at the end of the week? When you're done, indulge in a favorite TV show, book, or relaxation pastime (reward). This exercise helps you in **Finding Your Flow**.

Developing Your Strengths

Can you make using your strengths a priority each day? After all, as Will Durant famously suggested: "You are what you repeatedly do. Excellence, then, is not an act, but a habit." The good news is that when it comes to developing your strengths, studies suggest that small, regular actions are the best way to create lasting change. In fact, finding new ways to use your strengths each day has been found to help increase your levels of happiness, confidence, and engagement, and lower your levels of stress.

How can I develop my strengths each day?

When you break the changes you want to make into tiny, busy-proof steps, you stop feeling overwhelmed and exhausted, and instead start adding up success after success. In particular, studies suggest that mindfully focusing in an open, curious, and nonjudgmental way on the strengths you're using effectively can provide you with the motivation to use your strengths more consistently. Then, as your confidence grows and your fear of failure withers, your progress accumulates into a spiral of positive behaviors.

What can I try?

- **Use Your Strengths In A New Way:** As you plan your day, select one task that will allow you to intentionally use one of your strengths in a new way. If there isn't a task that's a good match, then think of one thing you can do today to develop a strength you'd like to build or explore.

- **Take A Mindful Strengths Pause:** As you move between activities, try to take a moment to briefly pause, take a few deep, slow breaths, and then ask yourself: "Which of my strengths will I bring forward now?"

- **Invest In A Daily Strengths Habit:** Harness your brain's neurological habit loop of cue, routine, and reward to create a daily strengths habit. For example, to develop your strength of creativity: When you sit down for your morning coffee (cue), spend ten minutes brainstorming possible solutions to a problem or opportunity you are facing (routine), then share your three best ideas with another team member (reward).

Is there a habit I can play with?

Each morning when you get to work (cue), write down one task you'll tackle today that can draw upon your strengths (routine), then grab your morning coffee or tea (reward).

Being Mindful

Do you ever find yourself mindlessly eating, driving, or working, only to realize later that you're not entirely sure how you completed this task? Our minds often wander—ruminating on the past, worrying about the future, or drifting here and there. Mindfulness is the ability to be fully aware, nonjudgmental, and curious about each moment in your life—what you are thinking, feeling, and doing in the here and now. It's the simple act of being present for what's happening in and around you. Studies have found that being mindful can help you to improve your self-awareness, acceptance of yourself and others, your ability to handle stress, and your wellbeing.

How can I develop more mindfulness?

Practicing mindfulness involves training your mind to focus on the moment, with openness and curiosity for whatever unfolds in the experience—your thoughts, feelings, and the actions of others. You can do this by giving your full attention to whatever you are doing at the moment, whether it's eating your lunch, driving to work, or attending a business meeting. You can also boost the ability of your mind to focus on the present moment through regular meditation practice. Studies also suggest that mindfully focusing in an open, curious, and nonjudgmental way on the strengths you're using effectively can provide you with the motivation to use your strengths more consistently. And if you find your mind wandering, rather than beating yourself up, recognize this as an opportunity to recommit to building your mindfulness "muscles" and gently bring your attention back to the present.

What can I try?

- **Eat Mindfully:** At least once a week, eat one of your daily meals mindfully. Choose a quiet, relaxed area to eat alone and remove all distractions if you can. Be curious about what you're eating. Approach it as if this is the first time you've ever really tasted this particular food. Begin eating slowly. Take a bite and taste and savor the flavors on all areas of your mouth. Chew while noticing the textures and consistencies. Swallow the food and follow its path into your stomach, then notice the feeling of being slightly more full. Every bite will be different; experience these differences. Observe and acknowledge any thoughts you may have, and continue to eat mindfully.

- **Look For What's Novel:** As you move through your day, try to actively notice new things, relinquish your preconceived beliefs, and then act on your new observations. We like to think of this as looking for gold. By opening your eyes and your mind to look for new ways of seeing what's unfolding right in front of you, can you discover new possibilities for learning, growth, connection, and joy?

- **Embrace Not Knowing:** When you think you have absolute answers, chances are there are contexts or ways in which you are wrong. For example, most of us would say that one plus one equals two. But this is not true if you're adding one wad of chewing gum to another wad of chewing gum, in which case one plus one equals one. Once you recognize that you don't know, you're more likely to start paying attention to what's happening around you. Instead of assuming that everyone knows something you should know but don't, try to remember that everything is always changing, things look different from different perspectives, and that there is no one way to know. So I don't know. You don't know. Nobody knows. And that means not knowing is just fine, so take the posture of being uncertain, confidently and mindfully asking the questions you need to uncover the potential truths in this context.

Is there a habit I can play with?

Take time to **Meditate Daily.** When you get ready to eat your lunch each day (cue), take two minutes to sit quietly and bring your awareness to your breath as you gently scan your body from head to toe and notice, without judging, how you're really feeling. Be sure to breathe a little more deeply into any parts of your body that feel tense, tight, or sore (routine). Then enjoy your lunch (reward).

Staying Playful

When was the last time you let go of feeling self-conscious, or your focus on getting a result, and just had fun? Researchers suggest that we are built to play and built through play, as it allows you to see things in a different way and explore new behaviors, thoughts, strategies, and ways of being that stimulate your brain for learning, growth, and creativity. As a result, playing can energize you, lift you out of the mundane, ease your burdens, renew your optimism, and open you up to new possibilities.

How can I develop more playfulness?

On one hand, play could be seen as purposeless. It's something you do voluntarily and for its own sake because whatever you're playing is inherently attractive and interesting to you. On the other hand, play could be seen as breaking free of constraints, allowing yourself to simply be. Give yourself permission to surrender to your curiosity and creativity as you improvise and explore new ways of doing things, losing track of time and any sense of self-consciousness in the process. Enjoy the fun of feeling actively engaged in what you are doing without the need for any bigger outcome.

What Can I Try?

- **Create Your Play History:** Spend time remembering what you did as a child that really got you excited and gave you joy—it might have been reading books, climbing trees, or backyard sports. Try to remember in as much detail as possible. Write down how these activities made you feel and ways you might be able to recreate these feelings in your job. Try not to be judgmental or skeptical. You can use these questions to guide you: When have you felt free to be and do as you choose? Is this part of your life now? If not, why not? How and why did some forms of play disappear from your repertoire? What might this mean for how you can create more moments of play now?

- **Be Playful:** Every day, find a way to play. It could be spending time with your pets, your children, or sharing a joke with someone. It could be finding small moments of creative play. Buy yourself some Legos, discover an online game you love, or undertake a new challenge just for the fun of it. It could be reminding yourself at work that one of the best ways to learn and innovate is to play and make time to experiment, to pull ideas apart, to get creative when it comes to problem-solving. Make time to play, knowing it is a pathway to growth.

- **Get Active:** One of the quickest ways to jumpstart play is to start moving. Consider setting up a play area at work that involves physical activities—like throwing a ball, playing with Velcro darts, or even bowling using a child-sized bowling game. Reach for these activities when you need a jolt of creativity or want to boost your playfulness as you interact with others.

- **Try Rapid Prototyping:** This is a playful and powerful way to bring your ideas to life—for products, services, processes, or experiences—in a visual and tangible process. Your rapid prototyping might include drawing a simple sketch, making a collage, building a simple model (using paper, cardboard, modeling clay or any other simple materials that can be glued or stuck together easily and quickly), role plays (for example, act out what an awesome customer experience would look like), creating a video, or creating customer avatar scenarios. Be as creative and playful as you wish.

Is there a habit I can play with?

After lunch each day (cue), spend ten to fifteen minutes playing with a new idea or approach simply for the joy of it. Don't be overly focused on the outcome. Simply use this as an opportunity to explore and great creative. You might want to have a sketchpad, box of Legos, or other tools to explore the activity with your hands, rather than just your head (routine). Then add a gold star to your to-do list or play chart to celebrate the time you've taken to be more playful (reward).

CHAPTER 4

Nurturing Positive Relationships

Positive psychology is a young field. While there is a growing evidence base around what works and what doesn't, there's a lot we are still learning. One consistent finding to date however, is the overwhelming importance of positive social relationships. As Professor Chris Peterson, one of the cofounders of the field, repeatedly noted, "other people matter."

A sense of belonging correlates with a range of positive outcomes, including higher self-esteem, greater life satisfaction, faster recovery from disease, lower levels of stress, less mental illness, and a longer life. Loneliness, social isolation, and the lack of social support place a person at high risk for psychological distress, physical and mental illness, and early mortality.

This is why, research suggests that more than what you're doing at work, it's who you're doing it with that ultimately determines your levels of engagement and wellbeing. For example, if you have a best friend at work, you're seven times more likely to be engaged in your job, produce higher quality work, and have higher levels of wellbeing. Furthermore, it's also less likely that you'll be injured on the job.

This is because you have a biological need for social support and each time you joyfully connect with another person, the pleasure-inducing hormone oxytocin is released into your bloodstream, immediately reducing anxiety, and improving your concentration and focus. In fact, studies have found that each positive interaction you have during the course of a work day actually helps to return your cardiovascular system back to resting levels, and over the long-term, this protects you from the negative effects of job strain.

Not only that, but when you experience warm and trusting feelings toward another person, it improves your vagal tone. This is the very subtle arrhythmia that occurs with each breath you take. It helps to calm your naturally high heart rate, regulate glucose and cardiovascular health, regulate your attention and emotion at work, and helps you have better social skills.

Professor Jane Dutton, of the University of Michigan, explains that the positive interactions we experience at work help us meet the deep psychological needs we all share to feel respected, valued, and appreciated. She calls these encounters "high-quality connections" and a growing body of research is finding that these moments contribute to individual flourishing and to team and organizational effectiveness.

The good news is that Professor Barbara Fredrickson's research has discovered that it takes just a micro-moment of genuine connection to spark an upward spiral of mutual care between people. Her research suggests it takes three simple steps:

- The sharing of a positive emotion, such as interest, joy, amusement, or pride.

- The synchronization of your biochemistry and behaviors through shared eye contact, or matching your body gestures or vocal tone.

- A reflective motive to invest in each other's wellbeing that brings about feelings of warmth and trust.

Fredrickson describes this process as "positivity resonance" and suggests that you think of it like a mirror. You and the other person mirror the positivity in each other's emotional state. You mirror each other's body and brain activity. You mirror each other's impulse to care for one another.

In these moments, you each become the reflection and extension of the other, truly making two heads better than one.

Unfortunately however, not all our interactions with each other at work are positive. Associate Professor Christine Porath, of Georgetown University, has found that ninety-eight percent of people report experiencing uncivil and rude behavior at work. Her studies suggest that people who are targets of incivility at work spend an inordinate amount of time worrying about the incidents, resulting in a depleted immune system, causing cardiovascular disease, cancer, diabetes, and ulcers. For example, a 2012 study by the Harvard School of Public Health, which tracked women for ten years, concluded that stressful jobs were just as bad for women's health as smoking and obesity.

Unfortunately, workplaces don't always make it easy to create positive connections with each other. Mistakenly believing that people will work harder to prove themselves when pitted against one another for limited resources and opportunities, they encourage cultures of cutthroat competition, rather than connected collaboration. Yet, Professor Adam Grant, of Wharton Business School, and his colleagues have found that when employees invest in effective high-quality connections and behave like "givers" rather than "takers" they are more efficient at solving problems, getting their work done, and balancing their workloads to ensure consistent performance. They build teams that are cohesive and coordinated and establish environments in which customers and suppliers feel that their needs are the organization's top priority. As a result, they have higher levels of profitability, productivity, and customer satisfaction, along with lower costs and turnover rates.

Good relationships take time and energy to develop and maintain—but are well worth the effort. Making time to genuinely connect with others is good for you and good for others. In an increasingly disconnected society, people long for others to care. Seemingly small acts of kindness or rudeness have been found to ripple through our networks at work and follow us home to the people we love. How are you shaping your relationships?

Michelle's Story: The Opportunity For An Introvert

As a natural introvert with a heightened level of social anxiety, after attending seven different schools as a child, finding ways to genuinely and warmly connect with others is not something that has come easy to me. My idea of hell is a roomful of strangers, and I spent a long period of my life swearing I was an island who needed nobody.

To be perfectly honest, discovering that when it comes to improving our wellbeing, the idea of "other people matter" didn't sit very comfortably with me. But after taking a deep breath and trying to see this as an opportunity that might finally ease my sense of isolation and loneliness when I was surrounded by others, I began gently playing with some of the ideas researchers were discovering.

Wanting to start small, I began by trying to create some micro-moments of positivity resonance with others by asking appreciative questions that helped me to discover the true, the good, and the possible in people. Instead of asking, "How are you?" I started playing with, "What's been the best part of your week so far?" Or, "What's coming up that you're looking forward to?" I found that in almost every case these questions opened up opportunities for people to share real stories with me about what was happening in their lives that I could genuinely connect to. As we savored the positive emotion ignited by these stories, sure enough, it set off upward spirals of warmth and trust that turned strangers into people I genuinely wanted to spend time with.

I also found it really powerful to understand that in every room where people gather, there is normally pain, and it's a gift that you give by seeing and being willing to sit with a person's pain when it's needed. It got me out of my own head about all the ways I didn't fit in or wasn't living up to people's expectations, and helped me to really start seeing the people in front of me and being able to reach out to others.

As I started to notice people's pain, I also couldn't help but begin seeing the strengths people also brought into the rooms where I worked—those moments where they were lit up, energized, and enjoying what they were doing. In each conversation, I started challenging myself to spot the best in people and to reflect this back to them, so that I could help meet the deep psychological need we all share of being respected, valued, and appreciated.

When I'd mastered the basics, I stepped it up to whole new level and embraced Professor Adam Grant's research on being an effective giver. I am honored to say that "generous" is the word I most often hear about my work. I feel truly humbled and grateful to have discovered that giving and being of service to others is actually what made my work and life feel meaningful. It turns out that other people really do matter after all.

Peggy's Story: Butterflies

Butterflies are one of my favorite creatures. When I was sixteen years old, Bob Carlisle released a song called "Butterfly Kisses," which has a line about a sixteen-year-old girl caught between trying to be a mature teenager and still being Daddy's little girl. It became a special song for me and my Dad—I was his butterfly kisses girl.

When I was in college, I got a butterfly tattoo on my back—a reminder that even though I felt like an ugly caterpillar at the time, one day I would find my wings and soar. I did, and these days as I fly around the world, one of my favorite airports is in Singapore, where they have a butterfly garden. You can walk into a magical world with butterflies fluttering all around you, filling the air with their gentle beauty. And every so often, when I'm walking through a field or a park, a butterfly flits by, and I think of it as a kiss of heaven lighting up my day.

I've always struggled with relationships. Growing up, I was shy and reserved. I had some good friends, but when forced to change schools, I found it hard to make new friends. I never seemed to fit in and was bullied by a couple of girls who were struggling with their own pain and saw me as an easy target. Day after day, I came home from school in tears, feeling lost and alone. I became convinced that there was something wrong with me.

I continued to struggle through school, longing to connect but never really feeling like I belonged. I threw myself into my school work and sports, succeeding as a student, but continuing to fail socially. Gradually, as I got older, I realized that perhaps I wasn't the only one who found connecting with others challenging.

As I started looking beyond the images people portray and listening more carefully to their stories, I began to notice that we all experience moments of sorrow and rejection and that this is part of the human condition. Instead of worrying so much about what people thought of me, I started looking for the best in each person, believing that there is always good to be found, even if sometimes it's hidden behind a hard core. Each of us is a special butterfly.

Over the years, many butterflies have come and gone in my life. Each place I have lived is like a different butterfly garden. For a period of time, I got to know the people there and then I travelled on with beautiful memories of how they filled the air around me. Some I will see again, others I never will.

Some butterflies exude a natural beauty, others are bruised and broken—beautiful in their own way, but in need of kindness and care. Perhaps that's how I feel at times—like a butterfly with a broken wing, just longing for a kind soul to see me as I really am. And so I try to be that person to others, for whatever time that special butterfly is in my life.

Nurturing Positive Relationships Toolkit

Being Compass-ionate	Listen Empathet-ically	Offer Micro-Moves	Be Available	See The Pain In The Room
Investing In Trust	Map Your Trust Bank	Give Away Control	Ask For Input	Delegate Daily
Giving Effectively	Perform Five-Minute Favors	Communicate Powerlessly	Chunk Your Giving	
Letting Go And Forgiving	Find Meaning	Build Your Forgiveness Muscles	Show Mercy	Forgiveness Moments
Sharing Good Times	Ask Appreciative Questions	Respond Actively And Constructively	Look For Strengths	
Navigating Incivility	Value Civility	Take Control	Gain Clarity	

Being Compassionate

Do you notice when others are in pain at work? It might be due to the pressure of unreasonable deadlines, feeling unappreciated for their efforts, navigating changes, being uncertain about their future, or challenges at home. Researchers suggest that you can safely assume that there is pain in every room in your organization. Pain colors the way you think, feel, and perform at work. This is why Professor Jane Dutton, Monica Worline and their colleagues are finding that when you practice compassion—your felt and enacted desire to alleviate suffering—you're likely to improve your resilience and adaptability in the face of change, be more engaged and committed to your organization, have better relationships with your clients, and provide a higher quality of service—which in turn increases people's loyalty to your brand.

How can I develop compassion?

Try to notice the suffering of others. As many people can feel too embarrassed or ashamed to talk about what's causing them pain, you need to keep your eyes open for changes in people's usual behavior. For example, they may appear exhausted, distracted, disengaged or short-tempered. By gently inquiring how they are doing, you can provide them a safe environment to explain what's happening for them. If they decide to share what's happening, generously interpret their suffering by not blaming or critically judging. Remember that while you may feel you can't do anything to solve their problem, just being there for them in the present moment can be enough. Any small thing you can offer may make a difference—a simple act of kindness can make a big difference to a person's sense of belonging, support, and self-worth.

What can I try?

- **Be Available:** Try to make yourself physically, mentally, and emotionally available to others. This may mean keeping your office door open whenever possible, arriving early or leaving later from meetings, spending time in the breakroom, or periodically taking a walk around your workplace and observing how people are doing.

- **Ask R U OK?:** There can often be the perception in the workplace that personal problems and challenges should stay out of the office. Yet those problems show up in how the person feels and functions at work. If you are concerned about a coworker, the simple question, "R U OK?" can open up a conversation and opportunity to show that you care.

- **Listen Empathetically:** When someone is telling you about a difficult situation or challenge, give them your full attention without interrupting or feeling you need to jump in with advice or to try to fix or solve their problem. Actions speak louder than words, so be mindful of what your behaviors are conveying to the other person. Try to be aware, non-judgemental, and curious about their story. Approach the conversation with kindness and compassion, with no other goal than improving your relationship with them and your understanding of what's happening.

- **Offer Micro-Moves:** Small actions or gestures don't have to take a lot of your time or energy but can make a huge difference in helping someone feel like their suffering is acknowledged. It might be offering to help with their workload, checking in with them regularly to see that they're managing okay, or giving them a small gift or card to cheer up their day.

Is there a habit I can play with?

Pay attention and **See The Pain In The Room.** When you arrive at work each morning (cue), take the time to really look around at your colleagues and notice if anyone seems to be in pain or suffering and give them your full attention as you check in with them (routine). Then, get your morning coffee or tea (reward).

Investing in Trust

How much do you invest in building a sense of trust with others? Studies have found that trust is fostered by acting with integrity, dependability, and good intentions. Trust can be hard to build and easily broken—especially for those with broken relationships in the past. Unfortunately, due to your natural wariness about trusting others, you may often adopt a "prove it" stance, making people earn your trust and holding back until they do. But you convey and earn trust most readily when you give others the benefit of the doubt, assuming people are trustworthy until they are found to be otherwise. This means taking a risk by making your vulnerability and reliance on others more visible. It is possible they will let you down and hurt you in the process, but it is more likely that you will sow the seeds of a positive relationship.

How can I develop more trust?

Trust is built upon honesty and integrity. Researchers suggest that you can build trust by sharing valuable information and resources, giving away control and responsibility, soliciting and acting on people's input, and communicating openly about issues that matter. These actions help to build a sense of "we're in this together," instead of "me against you." You also create trust by the things you do not do or say—including not accusing others of bad intent, demeaning others, micromanaging, surveillance, punishing people for errors, or sharing things told to you in confidence (unless there is potential harm to that person or to another).

What can I try?

- **Map Your Trust Bank:** On a piece of paper, place yourself in the center and then mind map around yourself the individuals and groups who trust you. What are you doing to maintain your high-quality, trusting connections with these people? If you find that your trust bank has gaps, it is time to consider action to build trust investments with these people.

- **Give Away Control:** You signal trust when you delegate decisions and tasks, especially when doing so means you must rely on others to bring about results that affect your own fate. Especially if trust is an issue, start small. Every day, try to delegate one thing on your to-do list to others. Take note of how this impacts your relationships and wellbeing.

- **Ask for Input:** Sincerely soliciting others' input is a powerful way to build trust. When you seek the input of others, you demonstrate your trust in their knowledge and skills. And, if you can act on what you hear, you send a powerful message of faith in them, while at the same time enhancing their trust in your sincerity.

- **Communicate Openly:** Be open and honest with others. Be willing to be vulnerable and admit to your weaknesses, especially when your personal experiences can serve as an example for others. Consider what information may or may not be appropriate for different audiences, when it's appropriate to share this information, and the best medium to use (face-to-face, telephone, email, etc.). You might share only vague details with some and greater details with others, but the key is to give a sense that you are not hiding things from others.

Is there a habit I can play with?

When you prepare your to-do list (cue), find one task (or part of a task) that can be delegated or have input from others to build trust with them (routine) and **Delegate Daily**. Then, use the spare time this has created to learn more about a topic you love (reward).

Giving Effectively

When it comes to your interactions with others at work, are you a giver, taker, or matcher? These preferences aren't about money, but about the attitudes and actions that shape your interactions with others. A growing body of evidence suggests that they play as much of a role in your success as hard work, talent, and luck. For example: In giver mode, you look for ways to be helpful to others; in matcher mode, you trade evenly with others; and in taker mode, you focus on getting as much as you can. And while being a taker might be good for the 100-yard dash, studies suggest that being an effective giver will improve your efficiency at solving problems, getting work done, and balancing your workload to ensure consistent performance.

You can test your relationship preferences at **www.adamgrant.net/ selfgivertaker**

How can I develop my ability to be an effective giver?

Researchers suggest that effective givers do three things differently. Firstly, they set boundaries around when, how, and to whom they give, so that they don't burn themselves out. Secondly, they are willing to ask for help when they need it, rather than worrying about imposing on others. Finally, they look for win-win-win outcomes that grow the pie for everybody, rather than being so ready to give that they end up wasting resources.

What can I try?

- **Perform Five-Minute Favors:** Spend five minutes each day helping someone else in your network. You could share information, connect contacts, offer feedback, or make a recommendation. If people offer to repay you in some way, ask them to pay it forward instead, by helping or supporting someone else.

- **Communicate Powerlessly:** Try not to dominate conversations by exerting your expertise at the expense of others. Instead, create win-win outcomes when you communicate by seeking people's advice, asking questions about their needs, and softening your assertions so everyone has a chance to contribute to the conversation.

- **Chunk Your Giving:** Balance your giving with other commitments by setting aside a specific time each week to give. Align what you're giving with the strengths you have and the needs you can see around you. For example, you could help on a project, mentor someone, or connect people in your network.

Is there a habit I can play with?

When you prepare for a meeting (cue), write down at least two questions you can ask that will allow others to share their expertise and contribute to the conversation (routine). Afterwards, give this meeting a big star on your calendar (reward).

Letting Go And Forgiving

Do you readily forgive others? Unfortunately, harm, abuse and injustice are common occurrences in workplaces. They frequently lead to retribution, condemnation, victimization, and revenge; as a result, researchers have found that individual performance and wellbeing almost always deteriorates. Studies suggest, however, that learning to forgive can help you to feel less hateful, hostile, and anxious, and be more compassionate with others.

How can I develop more forgiveness?

Researchers recommend letting go of grudges by viewing the people who have wronged you with compassion and by remembering that most of us are doing the best with what we have at any moment in time. You can also try looking for possible benefits of their hurtful actions; for example, perhaps they helped you learn and grow, helped you be more understanding of others, or to free yourself of anger. While you don't need to forget or excuse the offenses, you do need to choose not to let their actions control your emotions. As the maxim notes: "Resentment is like drinking poison and expecting the other person to die."

What can I try?

- **Find Meaning:** Spend twenty to thirty minutes writing about a recent transgression you experienced. Consider the personal benefits of this experience. What did you learn? How does it add to your growth and ultimate wellbeing? Is it really worth holding on to and not forgiving the other person? Can you define this event as an opportunity to move forward?

- **Build Your Forgiveness Muscles:** Make a conscious effort to not talk disparagingly about those who have hurt you. You don't have to say good things, but if you refrain from talking negatively, it will feed the more forgiving side of your mind and your heart.

- **Show Mercy:** For two minutes, bring your focus to the gentle and consistent awareness of your breath as it enters and leaves your body. Now, bring to mind a person who has hurt you and you wish to forgive. Think of them as a whole person who behaved badly, rather than defining them solely by the offending behavior. Even if you don't wish for this relationship to be repaired, try to genuinely focus your thoughts and feelings on sending a gift of mercy or compassion to this person.

Is there a habit I can play with?

Have **Forgiveness Moments**. On your way home from work (cue), notice if anyone has caused you pain today and if you're feeling resentful toward this person. If you are, try to see them as a person who behaved badly today and forgive them this moment of human learning. Make a note if you need to do anything tomorrow to acknowledge or resolve the situation with them (routine). Then, walk in your front door knowing you are free from grudges and ready to begin your evening (reward).

Sharing Good Times

Are you making your connections with others count? Researchers have found that high-quality connections don't necessarily mean a deep and intimate relationship, and they don't require personal knowledge or extensive interaction. In fact, any point of contact with another person can potentially be a high-quality connection. One conversation, one email exchange, or one moment of connecting in a meeting can leave you and the person you've connected with a sense of vitality and benefit the wellbeing and performance of you both.

How can I develop better connections?

Studies have found that you can nurture high-quality connections by engaging respectfully with others by being present, listening actively, being genuine, and conveying affirmation. You can also help to engage others more in tasks by sharing information, advocating for others, being accommodating to improve their performance, and nurturing their success.

What can I try?

- **Ask Appreciative Questions:** Intentionally look for the *true*, the *good*, and the *possible* in others by flavoring your interactions with an appreciative inquiry. Ask questions such as: "What's working well right now?" and "What's been the highlight of your week?" or "What are you looking forward to in the coming months?" Savor the positive emotions you both experience as they share their story and invest in the feelings of warmth and trust.

- **Prioritize Friendships:** Research suggests you need at least one close friend that you can really count on—and several are even better. Identify three relationships you would like to invest more time in. For each of these, create a ritual (to perform on a daily, weekly, or every two weeks basis) that ensures you are regularly in touch. You might choose to head to the gym together, pick a new restaurant to try, or even have a regular telephone conversation. Remember to ask your friend for their input when creating the ritual, and give them space when required.

- **Respond Actively And Constructively:** When someone shares good news with you, slow down and take a moment to ask them some active and constructive questions to help them appreciate their good fortune and to gain more information about their experience. For example: "The promotion sounds so exciting. How did you find out? When will you start? What are you most looking forward to?" Such questions open up a conversation, and show the other person they are understood, validated, and cared for. As a result, our feelings of commitment and satisfaction in the relationship are enhanced.

- **Look For Strengths:** Enter your next work meeting wearing "strengths goggles"—and looking for the moments when your colleagues are at their best. You might notice a colleague asking lots of questions (curiosity), collaborating on a project (teamwork), or entertaining the group with a funny story (humor). After you spot their strength(s), if the timing is right, tell the person what you saw and why you value their strengths.

Is there a habit I can play with?

When you arrive at work (cue), take the time to ask someone an appreciative question and be fully present as they answer. Invest in the feelings of warmth and trust that arise between you (routine). Then, bask in the positive emotions you're enjoying with a funny cat video on YouTube or something else that makes you smile (reward).

Navigating Incivility

Are you struggling to cope with incivility at work? From answering calls or emails in the middle of a meeting to public belittling, taking others for granted, and flat out sabotage, Associate Professor Christine Porath suggests that incivility appears to be on the rise in our workplaces. Whether it's the cultural pressures of globalization, generational differences, the general fraying of workplace relationships, or the increased use of technology, we seem to be more focused on ourselves and less on others, not due to malice but a lack of self-awareness. Unfortunately, studies have found that this kind of workplace tension affects your mind in ways you might not even be aware of, disrupting your ability to pay attention, impairing your creativity, and robbing you of productivity. Left unchecked, these behaviors can damage your health, destroy your relationships, and leave you feeling depressed, anxious and burned out.

How can I better navigate incivility?

Think of rude behavior as a virus you need to protect and inoculate yourself from, so you don't get sucked into its contagious cycle. When someone is uncivil to us, we often have a tendency to either outwardly react—resulting in arguments, fights, and escalated conflict—or inwardly recoil—withdrawing, belittling ourselves, and building resentment. It's important to acknowledge when you feel hurt, and find appropriate ways to deal with your emotions. Researchers suggest it's important you don't let someone make you a smaller version of yourself. Instead, take a deep breath, gather yourself, refuel, stand tall, and play big. Consider what might have triggered their behavior—is it something you did, or could it be something going on in their life? If someone is often uncivil toward you, try to minimize the time you spend with them. Spend time instead with energizers—the people in your life who make you smile and laugh and make you feel good about yourself. Pour your energy into being kind to others rather than ruminating on the unkind of people. And focus on self-care—supporting yourself physically and mentally, as you ride the storm.

What can I try?

- **Value Civility:** Regardless of how well-behaved you think you are, we can all be a little kinder and more considerate. Take Associate Professor Christine Porath's quiz at **www.christineporath.com/assess-yourself/** to gain insight into your own behavior and then master the basics of smiling more, acknowledging people, and listening effectively to make your workplace more civil.

- **Take Control:** Help bring closure to uncivil behavior by journaling about what has occurred, thinking through the emotions you experienced and then choosing to let them go. Remember: you can visit "pity city," but you can't live there. Then, invest your energy in new learning opportunities that boost your sense of self and focus your attention on the things that are within your control. For example, find a great mentor to guide you, re-craft parts of your job around your strengths or people who energize you, or take up a new hobby or sport.

- **Gain Clarity:** In every interaction, you have a choice to lift people up or hold them down. You are going to be judged by the little moments. To make the most of them, start each day by getting clear and answering this question: "Who do you want to be?" You have more control than you think—even in the face of the most uncivil behavior. Your attitude, mindset, and willfulness can make a difference. In each moment, you get to choose whom you want to be.

Is there a habit I can try?

When you travel to work (cue), take five minutes to reflect or journal on who you want to be today. How will you lift others up? How will you ensure you don't let people hold you down (routine)? Then celebrate by walking into work and immediately putting this into action (reward).

CHAPTER 5

Finding More Meaning

"Death is more universal than life;
everyone dies but not everyone lives."
~ *Andrew Sachs, British actor*

What drives you to go to work each day? Is it simply to pay the bills and survive, or are there deeper reasons—to support your family, to change lives, and somehow make a difference through what you do?

We spend much of our lives working. For decades, people have ranked having a sense of purpose in their work as more important than promotions, income, job security, or even flexible hours; yet, for many of us, finding meaningful work feels like something we just can't afford. While researchers have noted that people struggle to find meaning in their jobs when they lack autonomy, variety, challenges, feedback, and the chance to see things through from start to finish, the single strongest predictor of meaningfulness is the belief that your job has a positive impact on others.

When a sense of meaning is found in your work, a growing body of evidence suggests you'll be happier, more motivated, more committed, and more satisfied, which enables you to perform better. The fact is you have a universal need to feel that what you do matters, and that your hard work isn't wasted.

Researcher Emily Esfahni Smith suggests that meaning can be reached through a number of different paths. These include:

- Feeling like you belong to a tribe that values your contributions and provides opportunities for frequent pleasant interactions.

- A purpose that motivates you to be of service to others.

- Being able to create a story that helps you to make sense of your place in the world and craft a positive identity.

- Transcendent experiences that lift you above the everyday world to feel connected to a higher reality and something bigger than yourself.

The idea of meaningful work sounds good in theory, but can be a big ask for many of us. Unsure where to start, too many of us choose to sit back and wait, hoping to one day be struck by a bolt of inspiration that clearly lays out our path to meaningful work, and settling for the status quo in the meantime. And while we hate to be the bearer of bad news, researchers have found that this is rarely ever the case.

Instead, studies suggest your sense of meaning usually unfolds bit by bit. It is a journey that is discovered and revealed over time, not simply a single peak experience. It often starts with the discovery of your interests, followed by a period of learning and development, which becomes a lifetime of going deeper and stretching further.

For example, Steve Jobs wasn't struck with the idea of creating personal computers and music devices. He tinkered with electronics as a kid, dropped in and out of creative classes in college, and worked at Atari. Finally, after joining a computer club, he got inspired to build computers with great graphics interfaces and changed the way people interacted with technology around the world.

Professor Angela Duckworth of the University of Pennsylvania suggests that if you haven't found your passion yet, a good place to start is figuring out what actually interests you. What do you like to think about? Where does your mind wander? What do you really care about? What matters most to you? If money wasn't an issue, what would you choose to do and why? How might this help others? What do you love doing, are good at, and get lost in? And, in contrast, what do you find absolutely unbearable? If you find answering these questions hard, think back to your teen years when vocational interests commonly sprout.

If you can only think of even a small direction, give yourself permission to explore it. According to Professor Bill Damon at Stanford University, your interests are the sparks that will ignite your passion over time. Go out into the world and do something small with it and notice what happens and how you feel about it. Remember, interests must be triggered again and again, so find ways to make this happen. Keep asking questions, and let the answers lead you to more questions. Continue to dig. Ask others what they think you are good at, and consider what that reveals about you. And have patience. Allow time for your curiosity, knowledge, expertise, and confidence to carry you toward the things that you find are truly meaningful to you.

If you have lots of ideas, map them out, laying out the different pieces, seeing which interests connect together. This might identify areas that you are really passionate about, and might want to pursue further. Seek out other people who share a similar sense of meaning and purpose, and consider how you can live more according to that purpose. As your interests grow, see how others are using those interests to accomplish something that goes beyond themselves. Consider how you can also make a difference by using your interests in the service of others.

This doesn't mean you need to save the world—or even large parts of it—in order to find meaning in your work. Professor Amy Wrzesniewski of Yale University has found that no matter what your job description says, what you do each day can make a positive difference for others. What matters is how you think about the work that you do, not the task itself. For example, in one set of studies with hospital janitors—whose responsibilities were to sweep the floors, dust, and empty the wastebaskets—she found that they were equally likely to describe their work as a job that paid their bills, a career that would lead them to other opportunities, or a calling that helped people to recover from illnesses by ridding the hospital of dangerous germs.

Think of finding meaning in your work like the parable of the three men who were crushing stones. When asked what they're doing, the first replies, "Breaking big rocks into little rocks," the second says, "Feeding my family," and the third explains, "Building a cathedral." It turns out that a sense of meaning has little to do with your job description or occupation, and more to do with choosing to see the small daily differences you can make for others, how your work connects to a bigger picture, and how it can be an expression of your deepest interests and values.

Of course, like all the wellbeing tools we're exploring, it's important to use meaning in intelligent ways to improve your wellbeing. Professor Robert Vallerand, of the Université du Québec à Montréal, has found that our passions can be either harmonious or obsessive. When you feel in control of what you love doing, you have the kind of harmonious passion associated with higher levels of physical health, psychological wellbeing, self-esteem, and work satisfaction. But when your passion starts taking control of you and making it difficult to engage in other things or with other people, this is a sign that you have developed an obsessive passion. This leads to your self-esteem and self-worth becoming dependent on the outcomes of the passion, which can damage your relationships, undermine your wellbeing, and eventually lead to burnout. The key becomes finding the right balance between being led by and following your passions, and not letting them take control of you.

Michelle's Story: Keeping Passion Harmonious

When I finally left my soulless corporate job to do the work I love by teaching others how to build and maintain their wellbeing at work, I thought all my Christmases had come at once. After a career of climbing the corporate ladder, I'd jumped off to finally invest my energy in work that could make a real difference for others. It was a gift for which I felt overwhelming gratitude and it was my heartfelt hope that I could truly find a way to make a lasting difference for others.

I hit the ground running and began teaching workshops, coaching executives, and writing blogs and books. Having never run my own business before, it was a white-knuckle experience, as I tried to get my head around the creation of intellectual property, managing a website, and meeting my tax responsibilities. Fortunately, I loved what I was doing and got to see the positive impact it was having for others every day. So I kept running and running to learn more, do more, and deliver more to ensure I didn't waste the incredible gift I'd been given.

Before I knew it, almost five years had passed and while I still loved my work, I started to realize I was becoming exhausted by my efforts. I tried cutting back my hours, but the joy of delivering "just one more" workshop proved impossible to turn down. I tried spending more time with friends, but discovered almost my entire social circle was full of positive psychology practitioners who loved talking shop. I tried making more time for my family, but found that our lives were endless "teachable moments" to learn and apply the skills I was paid to teach others.

The problem I discovered is that when our passions light up our lives, and make us feel so competent, good, and alive, engaging in them becomes an easy compensation for what's missing in the rest of our lives. My sense of self-worth was becoming so contingent on being a wellbeing teacher who was helping to make a real difference for others, that unplugging had become almost impossible, as my passion began to consume every part of my life.

While a short sprint of obsessive passion seems to do little harm, I realized that I needed to find ways to start putting my passion aside and be present in other parts of my life. We started with a family piano and as I retaught myself the skills I'd long left behind in childhood, my kids came and sat alongside me to discover their own joy for music. I started sitting on the beach each day and watching the world pass for no other reason than the physical, mental, and spiritual space it gave me. I started truly investing in my sixteen-year-long marriage, rather than just rushing past each other as we tried to keep up with our lives.

My passion didn't become harmonious instantaneously, but these changes did begin to create more balance and energy in my life. I'd love to tell you I've nailed it, but I find that like the shifting tides, sometimes my passion is perfectly harmonious and other times there's still a little obsessive sprinting going on. The difference is that now I'm making conscious choices about how meaning is shaping my wellbeing.

Peggy's Story: The Journey of Life

Death is something we don't like to think about. It's something we fear, so we avoid the topic. But then our loved ones die, and it shakes our whole world. All that we know about how things are supposed to work is shattered, and it makes us question who we are and why we are here. It makes us come face-to-face with the reality that we are only on this planet for a brief time. And it begs the questions—what am I doing with my life, and does my life matter?

The topic of purpose in life has always rubbed me the wrong way. I've never had a clear idea on my purpose. People challenge us to identify where we are going and why. Where do you hope to be in five years? In ten years? I can't even begin to conceptualize what life will be. If you had asked me ten or twenty years ago where I'd be, I'd never have considered that I'd be an academic at the top university in Australia, working in positive psychology.

For better or worse, I view my life as an adventure. I don't know where it's leading me, but I embrace the journey, through the peaks and valleys that I encounter. I take opportunities as they come. On one hand, this makes my life story complicated because I haven't followed typical pathways—go to school, get a job, raise a family. And my career story is also complex—while I've published a lot of research, I'm not known for anything in particular because my research topics are all over the place. On the other hand, I've experienced many things that others never will. I have traveled the globe and lived abroad. I've worked with top scholars from around the world. I've experienced an exciting life that has opened up new possibilities and expanded my vision.

Either way, people come and go. Memories fade. Time moves on.

In the process of writing this book, my dear colleague, Christine, suddenly passed away. I only knew her for a few years, but she had quickly become one of my best friends. Christine was an incredible individual. She had a tremendous amount of energy. She was strong-willed, intelligent, and talked incessantly. We worked closely together to integrate the fields of positive psychology with her area of expertise—systems science.

She was happy. She loved her family, her job, and life in general. She did the tasks that were required of her, and went above and beyond the call of duty, always showing care and concern for others. And she had an incredible heart for the less fortunate. She was lit up by the idea of making a difference in the world.

Christine did not have a vision for her future. Like me, she let life happen, embracing the excitements and challenges that it offered. A true systems perspective—to have razor vision of one's path ignores the complexity of the reality all around us. And yet when people reflected on her amazing life, it was full of meaning. Her passion and courage made a clear impact on people. She had a heart of gold. She was a beautiful person, inside and out. She did not try to fit a particular image; she was simply herself—and that made all the difference. I am a different person because of the time that I was privileged to spend with her, and I know many others have benefited from her life.

And so I find myself reconsidering my purpose. Why am I here? I don't know the answer to that question. But I'd like to believe that by applying my passions, talents, strengths, and interests I can also make a difference in the world, even for just one person. And that would be enough meaning.

Finding More Meaning Toolkit

Investing In Belonging	Give At Work	Find Your Tribe	See Others	Create Coffee Dates
Creating Purpose	For The Sake Of What?	Make The Mundane Meaningful	Invest In SPIRE	Outsource Inspiration
Practicing Storytelling	Uncover Your Story	Be A Journalist	Release Your Lost Self	Find Redemption
Allowing Transcendence	Be Awed By Nature	Find A Spiritual Practice	Get Perspective	Savor Beauty
Making Passion Harmonious	Restore Balance	Cultivate Alternative Passions	Set Boundaries	Measure Your Passion

Investing In Belonging

Do you belong to a tribe? Researchers are finding that we all need to feel understood, recognized, and affirmed by others. We all need to give and receive affection. We all need to find our tribe. A sense of belonging has been found to be the most important driver of meaning, and yet, sadly, studies suggest that a sense of loneliness is on the rise as traditional forms of community are dissolving and leaving us feeling more isolated and alone. While you can't control if someone will show you understanding and affection, you can choose to initiate or reciprocate it. You can decide to say hello to people at work, rather than averting your eyes. You can choose to value people rather than devalue them. You can invite people to belong.

How can I build more belonging?

Researchers suggest that belonging is more likely to occur when your relationships are based on mutual care, love, and a sense of being valued. Focusing on others is the easiest way to build a sense of belonging. So reach out to the circle of people around you at work—your colleagues, your clients, and your suppliers—and look for ways you can improve their lives by playing on your unique strengths and interests. And it doesn't need to stop with the immediate circle of people you come into contact with. Spending money on others, giving to charity, or volunteering are valuable ways to boost your sense of meaning and wellbeing.

What can I try?

- **Give At Work:** Find out if your workplace has a workplace-giving program. This might involve sponsoring a charitable organization or events, or providing time to volunteer in the community. If so, commit to being involved in the program. If your organization doesn't have an established program, look for other meaningful opportunities to volunteer and help others in your workplace or in the community. If you can, make this a regular weekly or at least monthly activity.

- **Find Your Tribe:** Getting lost in the flow of an activity is far more enjoyable and meaningful when you experience it with others. Reach out to others by finding a group of like-minded people. You can start by considering your interests and passions and look for a group that focuses on these. Or you may want to join a group that gives you the opportunity to step out of your comfort zone and learn something completely new.

- **See Others:** We each long to be seen for the people we can be. Try looking people in the eyes, genuinely smiling and saying hello when you walk past them at work. Invite colleagues on a coffee date to learn more about them, the work they're doing, and what lights them up. Listen better by putting your phone away, suspending your judgements, and giving people your full attention. Make it your practice to really see others.

Is there a habit I can play with?

Create Coffee Dates. When you plan your week (cue), reach out to at least one person for a coffee date or quick lunch to catch up or get to know them better (routine). Then add this person's name to a mind map you have made of your tribe so you can see the connections you're building (reward).

Creating Purpose

Do you have a clear sense of purpose? Your purpose is the driving force behind who you are; it's the internal compass that motivates you to keep heading in the direction of how you want to live your life. It involves tapping into your deepest desires to contribute and to make a difference to something bigger than yourself. Without purpose, you can drift through life aimlessly. But with it, studies have found you'll be more motivated to accomplish the goals that matter most to you, and be resilient in the face of challenges.

How can I develop more purpose?

Researchers suggest that instead of approaching your purpose as a noun (something you either do or don't have), treat it like a verb (something you actively discover and develop). Finding your purpose means uncovering opportunities to put your passions into action right now. Rather than looking for that dream job, it's about creating opportunities that allow you to inspire, to teach, to empower and help people right where you are. Cultivate a service mindset that helps you to reframe the tasks that occupy your time into a way to help others. Then, make this choice your legacy.

What can I try?

For The Sake Of What?: Spend some time journaling, for as long as it takes, in one long burst or several short ones. When you think about the work you most want to do in the world, what lights you up? What would feel meaningful for you? It may be a stretch from where you sit right now, but if you're really honest, what is the work you would do even if nobody paid you to do it, or recognized you when you did? How can you start right now? Write about what you are willing to get out of your comfort zone for, to risk failure, to put your ego aside and truly show up. Then identify one small step you can take to start right now.

Make The Mundane Meaningful: Find more meaning in small tasks at work by creating a meaning map. Place a piece of paper horizontally on the table. On the left-hand side, write down a task that feels devoid of meaning. Then, draw an arrow to the right and ask: "What's the purpose of this task?" and "What will it accomplish?" Write down your answer. If what's written down still doesn't feel important enough to get you firing on all cylinders, then draw an arrow to the right once more and ask again what the purpose and outcomes are. Keep repeating this step until you find your own "aha" moment that makes it easy to see the bigger value of a little task.

Invest In SPIRE: Know your unique *Strengths* and talents and use them as you go about your work; *Personalize* your work by aligning what you do to your values; *Integrate* your motivation for your job in ways that bring meaning to the rest of your life; find ways to *Resonate* with your organization's core values and mission; and look for paths to *Expand* the benefits of your work for others.

Outsource Inspiration: Gain inspiration and meaning by connecting to the people impacted by the work you do. They may be people or groups internal or external to your organization. Try to learn more about the challenges they face and the differences your work can make in their lives. Keep the insights you gather somewhere you can see them regularly to remind you of the opportunity for meaning that you have.

Is there a habit I can play with?

On your way home from work (cue), take a few minutes to reflect on the difference you made for others today and note these down (routine). To celebrate, kick back with a favorite song, audio book, or podcast to relax (reward).

Practicing Storytelling

What are the stories you tell about your yourself and your life? Stories can help you to make sense of why things happen the way they do and your place in the world. They are how you make meaning in your life. Researchers have found that people living meaningful lives are able to step back from the daily details of their lives, and provide a broader narrative that makes sense of experiences they have had and how those experiences have made them who they are. For some, it is a story that transitions through suffering to growth. For others, there is connection and agency. This doesn't mean their lives have objectively improved, just that they've found meaning in what has unfolded for them and feel that they are in control of their lives and are progressing. In contrast, people who interpret their life or life events as going from good to bad tend to be more anxious and depressed.

How can I develop more meaningful stories?

You can edit, revise, and reinterpret the stories you tell about your life. Studies have found that even making small story edits can have a big impact on how you live. You may benefit from reflecting on pivotal moments in your life and explore the growth, connection, and choices you made to positively shape the outcomes. You may find it helpful to tell stories about the future where you can imagine that everything has gone as well as possible to ignite a sense of hope that pulls you into action. Some of us even find it helpful to tell the stories of our lost selves—the futures we've missed out on—to allow for closure and growth.

What can I try?

- **Uncover Your Story:** For as many days as it takes, spend at least ten minutes journaling in a stream of consciousness about something that has happened to you and how you're feeling about it. Don't overthink it, don't edit it, just let it pour out. This can give you the space you need to understand and come to terms with what is unfolding.

- **Be A Journalist:** If you are experiencing stressful or challenging circumstances, look at the events as if you were a journalist. How would a journalist describe the situation? What would they identify as turning points in your life, a moment when you found meaning and stronger purpose? What would they find if they followed you for a week? What examples of your strengths and resilience would they see? What photos would a photojournalist take to demonstrate your growth, values, and strengths? Take time to write your own story (in any medium). You don't need to share this with anyone.

- **Release Your Lost Self:** Spend about fifteen minutes writing about your best possible self and how you had hoped your life would unfold if everything went as well as it possibly could have. Then, spend about fifteen minutes writing about your lost possible self, the "self that could have been," had you not encountered the difficulties you've faced. In both cases, try to be as detailed and specific as you can. Although writing about your lost self can be painful, studies have found this exercise can help you to reconcile the loss and leave a more positive mark on the life you've ended up living.

For each of these exercises, after you finish, take time to read through that story. What themes come out? What does it reveal about your thoughts and perceptions? How does it fit within the broader picture of your life journey?

Is there a habit I can play with?

Find Redemption each night as you go to bed (cue); spend a few minutes writing or reflecting on a time a negative event has led to unforeseen positive consequences or new opportunities and what you learned from this experience (routine). Then go to sleep (reward).

Allowing Transcendence

When was the last time you felt truly connected to something bigger than yourself? Perhaps you witnessed a beautiful sunset, were inspired by a piece of music, were amazed by a kind act of human nature, or felt a sense of connection to a higher power? Researchers have found that transcendent states occur when your sense of self washes away, along with all your petty concerns and desires, and you feel deeply connected to other people and everything else that exists in the world. The result is that your anxieties evaporate, your generosity and concern for others increases, life finally seems to make sense, and you experience a deep state of peace and wellbeing.

How can I develop more moments of transcendence?

Studies suggest that transcendence is enabled by experiencing the state of awe. You feel awe when you notice and engage with something so grand and vast that you can't comprehend it, like a magnificent vista, exquisite art of any kind, extraordinary generosity, or the divine. You rise above the everyday to experience a higher reality that changes the way you understand the universe and your place in it.

What can I try?

- **Be Awed By Nature:** A considerable number of studies point to psychological and physical benefits of nature. Even as the sciences have progressed over the past few centuries, so much of the natural world goes beyond the human mind. As much as we try to control every aspect of our lives, nature is uncontrollable. Spending time in nature can provide perspective, reminding us that we are a part of a much bigger world. Find ways to regularly be awed by nature. It might be walking in a local park or on the beach, taking in the glory of the sky at different times of the day, or immersing yourself in a wilderness experience. Be mindful—use all your five senses to notice your surroundings as if it is the first time you are experiencing them.

- **Find A Spiritual Practice:** If you feel there is a higher power guiding you, then make time to connect, to reflect, and to absorb the sense of wonder, love, and purpose that this offers. It could be spending time in nature, with animals, at a sacred or religious place, a yoga class, or in prayer or meditation. Create the space to fuel this connection.

- **Get Perspective:** Find an experience that creates a sense of awe for you—be it sitting at the foot of a dinosaur skeleton in a museum, on a beach as the waves crash to the shore, or in front of a beautiful piece of art. Drink in its wonder, and then try to ask yourself the question: "Who am I?" Write twenty sentences, each beginning with "I am" and allow this to intensify your experience of awe.

Is there a habit I can play with?

When you sit down to eat your lunch (cue), take five minutes to write about your experiences of witnessing beauty—acts of moral excellence or courage, your reflections on nature, your responses to an elevating piece of music or art, or people's stories that have inspired you (routine). As you eat, savor these discoveries—**Savor Beauty**—and let yourself breathe in the wonder of what's possible (reward).

Making Passion Harmonious

Are you too passionate about your work? Feeling passionate about key activities can become a defining feature of who you are and can be what makes your life worth living. But a passion can become obsessive when it starts to make you feel so competent, good, and alive that it becomes a way to compensate for other things that are missing in your life, making it harder and harder to disengage from the activity. You start to eat, live and breathe your passion, unable to switch off. Researchers have found that while an obsessive passion is unlikely to do much damage in the short-term, over time it can take control of your life—putting you at risk of damaging your relationships, undermining your wellbeing, and eventually leading to burnout. On the other hand, when your passions are harmonious and you can put them aside and keep them in balance with other parts of your life, studies suggest you'll experience higher levels of physical health, psychological wellbeing, self-esteem, positive emotions, creativity, and work satisfaction.

How can I develop harmonious passions?

Being purposeful in choosing which passions to engage in, how you engage in them, and how you balance them with the rest of your life can keep your passions harmonious. Even positive activities that are good for you, such as yoga or hiking, only provide positive benefits when you have a harmonious passion for them. Intuitively, you know when a passion is becoming obsessive. Be mindful of the impact a passion is having on your relationships, your wellbeing, and your performance and adjust your commitments accordingly. Are you in control of your passion, or has it taken control of you?

What can I try?

- **Restore Balance:** Short bursts of obsessive passion rarely do any lasting harm, but when the milestone has been reached, it's important to rebalance your life and put your passion back into perspective. Remind yourself of the other things you love. Go back to your normal schedule. Revert to who you really are when life is harmonious.

- **Cultivate Alternative Passions:** Having more than one passion in your life will help you keep a passion from getting out of control. Each additional passion you cultivate outside of work gives you an opportunity to value the strengths you have beyond your job and lowers your chance of burnout. Think about what else interests you. What would you like to pursue purely for the joy of the activity? What lights you up outside of work?

- **Set Boundaries:** Avoid bringing your work home whenever you can. Leave your computer and those files that you didn't get to at work. Limit or don't check your work emails at home or while you're on vacation. Set an out-of-office message so people know they can't reach you.

Is there a habit I can play with?

At the end of your workweek (cue), **Measure Your Passion** by taking the time to imagine yourself as a pie and reflect on how big a slice your work has been this week. Has this served you well? Or would a smaller slice serve your wellbeing better? What can you do to bring this picture into better balance (routine)? Then go indulge a passion that has nothing to do with your work (reward).

CHAPTER 6

Amplifying Accomplishment

"Success is a journey, not a destination.
The doing is often more important than the outcome."
~ Arthur Ashe, American professional tennis player

Accomplishment means different things for different people. For some, it means acknowledged achievements—winning an award, outperforming the competition, or being promoted. For others, accomplishment is more subjective in nature—completing a task, feeling able to do what is expected of you each day, a sense of competence or mastery in your work, being proud of the work you do.

As a society, we often value the big achievements—the feats we can observe and applaud. We are inspired by those who are successful. A vision of what's possible can motivate us to stretch beyond our self-imposed boundaries. But they can also be demotivating. Successful people can appear to have special talents or come from privileged backgrounds. It's hard to imagine winning a Grammy when it's all you can do to meet the many demands of your family and work life.

From a wellbeing perspective, it is often the small, subjective wins that matter most. Indeed, big accomplishments feel good—they offer peak experiences and defining moments. But the glow quickly fades and we start looking for something bigger and better around the corner.

Professor Carol Dweck of Stanford University suggests that when it comes to accomplishing the things that matter most to you, more important than your abilities is the belief that you can improve. Regardless of your current ability, you can improve, with motivation and effort. In the words of Christopher Robbin: "You're braver than you believe, stronger than you seem, and smarter than you think."

This is not to say talent doesn't matter. It does. Talent, natural abilities, and your basic biological makeup define the range of what might be possible, but they don't guarantee it. If you are tone deaf, you probably won't become a musical virtuoso. No matter how much you train, you probably won't outpace the African runners in a marathon. But most of us do not know the upper limits of our potential. We settle within a comfortable range of what we believe is possible, rather than pushing the boundary of what could be possible.

What we perceive to be talent often is the result of a lot of hard work. For example, in a study of competitive swimmers, the very best performances were not purely a matter of extraordinary talent, but the confluence of dozens of very ordinary skills or activities that had been carefully drilled into habits, then synthesized into a whole. What made these performers extraordinary was the fact that they were able to consistently and correctly complete the required actions at the right time. Your willingness to exert effort and learn from your prior successes and failures is what ultimately turns talent into performance.

Unfortunately, Professor Angela Duckworth of the University of Pennsylvania explains that we tend to carry a hidden prejudice against those who've achieved what they have because they worked for it, and a hidden preference for those people we think arrived at their place in life because they're naturally talented. We're drawn to stories of overnight success, and conveniently ignore all the years of unrecognized, unappreciated hard work that carried the person to that success. If there is something special about those people, then it frees us from needing to try. We get distracted by talent and create stories that hold us back from achieving what we want most.

Researchers have found this naturalness bias robs you of the opportunity to pivot from "This is all I can do" to "Who knows what I can do?" It also robs you of the opportunity and joy of learning. When you expect instant perfection, this denies that making mistakes, bumping up against your limitations, building mastery over time, and falling short of your ideals are how you move toward your true potential. Instead of interpreting the inevitable obstacles, setbacks, and plateaus in your progress as signals to intensify your effort and practice and persist, you're more likely to see them as signals to quit.

The most successful people in any field rarely succumb to these thoughts of giving up. When it comes to mastering new behaviors, they have a ferocious determination. They're resilient and hardworking, and they know in a very deep way what they want. In what she calls *grit*, Duckworth suggests that the combination of passion and perseverance is what makes them high achievers.

That is not to say that those who are successful are gritty, or that the seemingly unsuccessful lack grit. Remember that high objective achievement is the dominant perspective of success. Many of the most successful people in the world experienced a certain degree of privilege along the way. Be it special talents, social class, socioeconomic resources, better schools, or pure luck, they often had opportunities others did not have. Perhaps that's why we are so inspired by stories of resilience—children who came from severe poverty, or experienced abuse and trauma, and yet turned their lives around. But even the most resilient did not succeed on their own. Parents, teachers, or other people saw something in them. Perhaps they made sacrifices, gave additional time and resources, or provided encouragement and support, that kept a ray of hope alive in the child.

The risk here is that we blame those who are unsuccessful for circumstances that are beyond their control. But we are also at risk of not taking responsibility for what is within our control. We settle for the status quo, saying that we simply aren't smart enough or it's the system's fault, not ours. The key is to go beyond what we may think is possible, while accepting that there can be real limitations. Talent, privilege, and luck all can breed accomplishment, but the question becomes what a person does when things get hard. Many people who seem unsuccessful in the world's eyes are extremely gritty. Take, for instance, the parents of a child with profound autism. For years, they watch their child struggle, face criticism by others as their child breaks social norms, and they give up their own dreams, doing all they can to minimize their child's suffering. They have more passion and perseverance than many of the seemingly successful.

Gritty people have a deep underlying belief that with effort, practice, and the willingness to learn, they can always improve. They focus on controlling what they can, and instead of simply setting performance goals for the outcomes they want, they prioritize learning goals that highlight the knowledge and skills they need to build to have the best chance of producing their desired results. This boosts their confidence to take on new challenges, to learn from criticism and feedback, to see failure as a teachable moment. Dweck describes this as a *growth mindset*.

Studies have found that a growth mindset makes it easier to set yourself stretch goals, to ask for help as you go, and to feel motivated to achieve the things that matter to you most. It sparks hope by helping you feel like you have nothing to lose and everything to gain if you step outside your comfort zone. It appears to help you move beyond your present limitations and to achieve your true potential. As Thomas Edison is quoted as saying: "I have not failed. I have just found 10,000 ways that won't work." So now, when we're in the middle of a good failure, we can remind ourselves that we're not up to 10,000 yet, and our light bulb moment might be right around the corner!

But can grit and a growth mindset backfire? Author Caroline Adams Miller writes of "stupid grit"—when you are consumed by obsessive passion and persevere at all costs, despite all the signs that you should stop. Similarly, Dweck recently told us that a growth mindset can go wrong when we persist with something to the detriment of the wellbeing of ourselves and others. For this reason, she believes that in addition to cultivating a growth mindset, it's important that we also practice self-compassion.

Dr. Kristen Neff explains that when your efforts to learn and accomplish the things that matter most to you don't go as planned, your brain is wired to protect you from pain and tries to attack the source of the problem. Which, in this case, is you! It fires up your inner-critic and feelings of self-doubt by telling you stories about why your efforts aren't working and what could go wrong to try and motivate you to push forward or to disengage entirely from the effort. Over time, this can heighten your stress and anxiety and undermine your confidence.

Self-compassion involves being mindful of the pain you're feeling, and reminding yourself that you're human, just like everyone else. It involves stepping away from your inner self-critic, and talking to yourself like a wise and kind friend. Would you say the things you say to yourself to a friend? Instead of taming, shaming, or blaming the voice of your inner-critic, self-compassion helps you to see things in a clearer and more balanced way so you can make informed choices about when to persist, when to try a different path, and when to let go and put your energy into something that will serve you better in the long-term.

As a result, studies have found that self-compassion helps you to generate more positive feelings that balance out your fears, allowing you to feel more joyful, calm, and confident. It helps you activate your brain's caregiving and self-awareness systems, making it easier to believe that you are capable and worthy, and making you less self-conscious, less likely to compare yourself to others, and less likely to feel insecure. And far from being self-indulgent or "soft," the deliberate use of self-compassionate talk has been found to be an effective means of enhancing your motivation, your performance, and your resilience.

Michelle's Story: The Power of Self-Compassion

I would have done anything to avoid walking out and giving a Pecha Kucha talk to 2,000 people at a recent conference hosted by the Dali Lama. For most of us, the idea of delivering a presentation to a group that large would be enough to have us

running home. But it wasn't the size of the crowd that I found terrifying; it was the fact that in a Pecha Kucha presentation, you have twenty slides, automatically timed to switch to the next one after exactly twenty seconds, with no way of stopping them. No clicker in hand. No technician to nod at. Once the clock starts, you just have to surrender and trust the process.

Listening to the audience applaud when the conference host introduced me, I realized there was only one way out. Despite my pounding heart, it was time to walk out onto that stage, to give it my best effort and accept that whatever happened—good, bad or anything in between—it would be the learning opportunity that I and everyone else in that auditorium needed that day.

When you watch the video of me presenting this talk, my words are perfectly timed to the slides, which automatically click forward every twenty seconds. Wanting to make the story I was sharing inspirational for others, I'd had the slides hand-drawn by an artist, and as the images began appearing, cameras popped up throughout the audience as people wanted to savor them. And while I was completely absorbed and present throughout the four minutes and twenty seconds I was on stage, my delivery wasn't as playful and engaging as when I'm teaching at my best.

Would I have loved the presentation to be perfect? Of course! Did I go home replaying all the words I slightly muddled and berating myself for being too nervous to loosen up and have more fun with it? Surprisingly (even to me), I didn't. Although letting my inner-critic run wild so that I never made those mistakes again would have been my instinct in the past, I have finally come to accept that success isn't actually about delivering the perfect result; it's about the willingness to stretch myself and take on new challenges, to show up and give it all my effort, and to have the self-compassion to learn from whatever unfolds. Of course, while that may sound very grown up, it's really just been a matter of finally figuring out how to work with my brain, rather than against it, so that I can have the best chance of accomplishing the things that matter most to me.

Peggy's Story: Achieving The Impossible

Marathons have been called the everyday person's Everest. The distance itself—26.2 miles—exceeds what the human body can do unless you build up your physical and mental capacity slowly over time. As a result, the moment you cross your first finish line you are changed forever. The impossible has become possible, and you realize that you can do far more than you ever imagined before.

It was New Year's Eve during my first year in graduate school when I set my first marathon goal. A friend of mine was planning on running the San Diego marathon in early June, and although I wasn't a runner, it sounded like as a good a goal as any to stretch toward. I went online that night and found a six-month training plan. I only had five months until the event, so I chopped off the first month and started running the very next day.

Many grueling training runs later, having built up my distance one slow mile at a time, I did successfully cross the finish line—swearing I would never run again. Until two weeks later, when I started dreaming of the next marathon.

I joined a running group. I started running more. And it became easier and more enjoyable. Soon, I was even calling myself a runner. It turned out that I was actually pretty good at running, so I started competing in races. And soon I had run the Phoenix, Boston (twice), and St. George marathons, each one faster than the last.

Finishing a marathon was no longer a stretch, and so I set myself a new goal of completing the next marathon in three hours and ten minutes. It was feasible, but I had to train harder than I ever had. But it was a challenge I was completely ready to take on.

Unfortunately, despite all my careful preparations and the two million spectators cheering me on, the race itself turned out to be an absolute failure. The day prior I'd walked all over New York eating the wrong foods and wearing myself out. It took four hours just to travel to the starting line, and overwhelmed by the 39,000 runners, I ran the first half too fast and by mile twenty-three my knee was hurting, I was walking and ready to quit. Eventually—well after my time goal had passed—I stumbled across the finish line, defeated, discouraged, and hyponutremic with my body literally shutting down.

I never wanted to run a marathon again, but decided I need to learn from my New York failure and give my time goal one last shot. I picked a marathon in Charlottesville, Virginia in which only several thousand people ran and started working with a running coach. It was an extremely hilly course which was going to make my time goal challenging so we added hill sprints to my training, mindfully managed my diet, and ensured my family was on hand to support my travel plans so I could arrive rested and ready to go.

It couldn't have been a more different experience from the New York marathon. As we headed out into the countryside, I found a running buddy from the crowd who had a similar pace and together we chewed up the miles, keeping ourselves fed and hydrated as required. As we neared the last few miles, he dropped behind, so with the crowds cheering me on I mentally pushed past the pain and maintained my steady tempo. As the finish line came into sight, my Dad's proud face appeared and before I knew it I was breaking through the ribbon as the clock showed the time of three hours and two minutes and tears of joy streamed down my cheeks. I'd set a course record and exceeded every expectation.

Today, I have no idea how I ran that fast for so far. It was a peak experience, which I know I can always look back on and be proud of what I achieved. But my favorite memory about that race isn't how well I ran it, or even my finishing time, it's the pride in my father's eyes at the lessons I learned through the training, the successes and the failures, and my ability to push myself beyond what I thought I was capable of accomplishing.

Unleashing Accomplishment Toolkit

Setting Goals That Work	Know What You Want	Audit Your Time	Stretch Yourself	Set Weekly Goals
Being Hopeful	Map Your Hopes	Start A Passion Project	Find Hopeful Friends	
Practicing Growth Mindset	Set Learning Goals	Get Comfortable With Failure	Name Your Fixed Mindset	Growth Mindset Reflection
Developing Grit	Draw A Grit Map	Ask For Help	Invest In Deliberate Practice	
Boosting Your Confidence	Strike A Power Pose	Take One Small Step	Acknowledge "Not Yet"	
Being Self-Compass-ionate	Create A Mantra	Write A Letter	Soothe Your Pain	Remember To Be Kind
Improving Your Resilience	Challenge Your Beliefs	Lean Into The Suck	Ban "Always"	Flex Your Stress Mindset

Setting Goals That Work

What type of goals are you working toward? Goals give you a standard to measure your progress and performance. Researchers have found that goals can provide you with motivation, help prioritize what you do, and are associated with higher levels of achievement. However, enjoying these psychological benefits depends on the type of goals you set. Although achieving a much sought-after goal can provide you with a burst of satisfaction, studies suggest that the pursuit of extrinsically-motivated goals—"have-to," "should-do," or "expected-of-you" goals—is likely to undermine your wellbeing in the long run. Instead, your wellbeing is better served by intrinsically-motivated goals—"want-to" goals that focus on opportunities for your learning and growth, connection with others, and sense of making a positive contribution. Also, it is often not the goals themselves, but the process of pursuing your goals that provides the greatest satisfaction. As Shakespeare observed, "Joy's soul lies in the doing."

How can I set better goals?

Firstly, consider why you are setting a particular goal. Researchers suggest it should pass the "so what?" test—what will come from achieving this goal and is this outcome truly important to you? Be clear on why your goal seems to matter. Is it driven by the opportunity to express yourself or to impress or appease others? Secondly, consider whether it should be a performance goal or a learning goal. A performance goal leverages your existing skills and resources to deliver an outcome you want to achieve. A learning goal helps you to build new skills and resources for things you hope to achieve in the future. Next, make your goal specific, challenging, and positive so it adds to your life, rather than subtracts from it. Include a tight deadline and a public commitment to enhance your motivation and performance.

What can I try?

- **Know What You Want:** Get clear on the goals you really want to pursue. Start by writing a list of all the things you can do when it comes to your work—these are the possibilities available to you. From these, circle just the ones that you really want to do. Then, reduce your choices further by reviewing the ones you circled and underlining those you really want to do. Finally, from the ones you have now circled and underlined, place a star next to the ones you really, really want to do—these are your deepest desires and wants. Now, create a plan for how to pursue these goals that matter most to you.

- **Audit Your Time:** At the end of each week, spend ten minutes writing down an overview of how you spent your time during the week. Ask yourself: "How can I spend more time on the things that matter most to me? Am I watching too much TV or spending too much time on the Internet? Am I saying yes to things that I should be saying no to?" Identify ways to reduce the time spent in activities that may be preventing you from achieving your goals, and spend more time focused on the goals you care about.

- **Stretch Yourself:** Creating SMART goals (Specific, Measurable, Attainable, Realistic, Time-bound) is a popular approach. The problem with this technique is that it encourages you to set low goals, instead of hard goals that are just beyond your grasp and provide you with the best opportunities for learning and growth. You can use this acronym to test whether your goals are well stated, but instead of attainable and realistic, shoot for wanted and difficult.

Is there a habit I can play with?

When you plan your week (cue), **Set Weekly Goals**. Make sure there is at least one "want-to" learning goal that is hard, specific, measurable, and has a tight deadline (routine). Then share your goal with someone who will give you accountability and support (reward).

Being Hopeful

Do you believe that tomorrow will be better than today and that you can make it so, even if there are challenges along the way? If you answered "Yes," then you have what researchers define as hope. Hope happens when your rational self meets your emotional self in the pursuit of clear "want-to" goals that excite you, with multiple pathways to help you navigate the obstacles (referred to as "way power"), and commitment to take the actions necessary to see them through (referred to as "will power"). As a result, studies have found that hopeful people are more effective problem solvers, use more coping strategies, feel more optimistic, and achieve more success. They are also likely to feel more satisfied with their lives, be more engaged, have better mental and physical health, and have a more confident outlook on life. They don't just believe in a positive future—they believe that they can make it a reality.

How can I develop more hope?

Researchers suggest that hope isn't innate, nor a by-product of your IQ. Rather, they have concluded that hope comes from your energy and excitement about what's next. It is created by setting "want-to" goals, mapping multiple pathways forward, and finding ways to maintain your willpower. Each of these parts work as a continuous feedback loop, setting the next part in motion, and forming a cycle that enhances your hope and optimism about the future. It is an action-oriented approach that takes control of your future and purposefully shapes it.

What can I try?

- **Map Your Hopes:** Take a sheet of paper horizontally and fold it into thirds. In the right column, write the heading "Goals" and write down a "want-to" goal you're genuinely excited to achieve over a time period that feels right for you. In the left column, write the heading "Pathways" and list at least three actions that could help you to reach your goal.

In the middle, write the heading "Obstacles" and for each pathway you listed, note obstacles or challenges you might encounter. Then, around the edges, or at the bottom of the page, add the things you can do to maintain your motivation and wellbeing, track your progress, and celebrate your efforts and achievements along the way.

- **Start A Passion Project:** Feeling excited and inspired about the future can help you get through the grind of everyday life. A passion project is something that excites you—it taps into your personal sense of meaning. It's not about the results, but the freedom of creative action and the experience of positive emotions. Identify a passion project that lights you up and spend at least ten minutes a day moving this "want-to" goal forward. It doesn't need a purpose; it just needs to be something that piques your curiosity and spurs your energy. It should elicit strong emotions. Spend some time mapping out your ideas. Set some specific goals, and identify what is needed to start the project. If you feel guilty at any point for indulging your passion, just remember that compared to typical scientists, Nobel Prize winners are twenty-two times more likely to perform as actors, dancers, or magicians; twelve times more likely to write poetry, plays, or novels; seven times more likely to dabble in arts and crafts; and twice as likely to play an instrument or compose music. So go ahead and indulge!

- **Find Hopeful Friends:** Hope is contagious, so find other people who are high in hope and spend regular time with them. Get inspired by their "want-to" goals. Learn from their stories to inspire you on how to maintain your hope in the face of obstacles and setbacks. Ignite your sense of willpower and excitement about what is yet to come.

Is there a habit I can play with?

Each morning before you start work (cue), spend at least ten minutes indulging in your passion project (routine). Celebrate your commitment by crossing this off your list for the day (reward).

Practicing Growth Mindset

Do you fear failure? The truth is, we all fail at something some of the time; the only question is whether we are learning from these experiences or missing out on some of life's best lessons because it feels too painful to admit we were wrong or didn't measure up. Researchers have found this response is often the result of a "fixed mindset" that is underpinned by the belief that you are born with a certain amount of talent and intelligence and that's your lot in life. People adopting a fixed mindset perceive outcomes as the ultimate measure of what people are capable of achieving—you're clever or dumb, good at sports or clumsy, musical or tone deaf. They also experience a heightened fear of criticism and perceive failure as a signal that they have reached the limits of their potential.

In contrast, people with a "growth mindset" believe that while you're born with a certain amount of talent and intelligence, with learning and effort you can always improve—and neuroscience now validates this belief. As a result, instead of just the outcomes, people adopting a growth mindset also value the learning and effort and are prepared to meet the challenges. This lowers their levels of stress and anxiety and gives them the confidence to reframe failure and criticisms as teachable moments that are as important to success as perfect outcomes.

It's important to note that we each have the capacity to sit in either of these mindsets—no one practices a growth mindset all the time. For example, you might have a growth mindset around the possibility of growing and learning in sport, but are convinced that you have no musical ability at all. Your mindset impacts how motivated you are to pursue different goals and whether or not you are willing to be open and flexible in your approach.

How can I develop a more growth mindset?

Studies suggest that the best place to start is to recognize how you think about your intelligence, abilities, and talents overall. Do you see them as open to development and growth, or something that is set in stone? What areas do you have a fixed mindset about, and which areas do you see as open to growth? Consider how you typically respond to failure or criticism from others. Then practice growing your growth mindset. Neuroscience is showing us that your brain creates new connections and strengthens existing ones as you repeatedly practice a skill and engage in learning and development. You can test this for yourself by setting a learning goal that focuses on improving your competence and pushes you beyond your comfort zone. When you fail or receive criticism, instead of beating yourself up or feeling ashamed, take a moment to celebrate your courage to try something you've not yet mastered. Embrace these as teachable moments and maximize the value of the learning they offer. If you have friends, family, or colleagues offering you praise or feedback, ask them to focus on your efforts and the processes they can see you using, so you can build on what's working, rather than chalking it up to luck or pure talent.

What can I try?

- **Set Learning Goals:** Each week, set at least one learning goal to build your competence in something. It might be a skill you want to gain, a task you want to master, or simply the desire to understand something better. Notice what happens as you practice, make mistakes, make adjustments, and eventually start to do better in the competence you're building. As you tackle this goal, practice letting go of the outcome, embracing your mistakes, and identifying the processes and efforts you can build upon to keep improving.

- **Get Comfortable With Failure:** Write down the three biggest mistakes or errors you've made at work in the last year. Next to each one, list the lessons or insights you gained from making these mistakes. Put the list somewhere handy so you can reread it when you need a reminder that mistakes can sometimes offer the best opportunities for learning and growth.

- **Name Your Fixed Mindset:** Give your fixed mindset voice a name. It might share the name of one of your parents, siblings, friends, teachers, or bosses. Start tuning into the stories this voice is telling you when you fear failure or criticism. For example, when you approach a challenge it might say: "Are you sure you can do this? Maybe you're not good enough?" When you hit a setback, it might say: "You see, I knew you couldn't pull this off, now everyone will know you're not as good as they thought." Or, as you face criticism, you might hear: "It's not my fault. That was never going to work!" Recognize that this voice is simply trying to protect you. But like a helicopter parent, it is overzealous in its effort, so try to talk back to it in a growth mindset voice. For example: "I don't know if I can pull this off, but I'll learn from the experience and I'll get better over time." Or, "Okay, I got it wrong. Let's own this failure and see what I can learn from the experience." Then take the growth mindset action.

Is there a habit I can play with?

At the end of each day (cue), ask yourself the following questions and write down your responses: What did I learn today? What mistakes did I make? What did I try hard at today (routine)? Then head home (reward) having completed your **Growth Mindset Reflection**.

Developing Grit

Are you gritty enough to achieve what matters most to you? When it comes to tackling our goals at work or in life, for many of us Professor Angela Duckworth suggests that: enthusiasm is common but endurance is rare. Let's face it, being gritty enough to see things through can be hard work, and yet, researchers have suggested that grit is a key predictor of success. Grit is the combined passion and perseverance for the pursuit of long-term goals. It's the ability to stick with working toward something for years, in the face of setbacks, disappointments, and plateaus in your progress. As the Japanese proverb suggests it's the ability to fall down seven times, and stand up eight. Studies suggest that it is associated with your levels of achievement, resilience, and wellbeing.

How can I develop more grit?

We are still learning how grit is cultivated. Researchers suggest that it can help to set meaningful goals, practice a growth mindset, cultivate hope through the stories you tell yourself, engage in both deliberate practice and moments of flow to improve your skill sets, and surround yourself with other gritty people who encourage you to stick to your goals. It's also worth noting that some goals may be more suited for grit than others—so pursuits that lead to observable and tangible results, like building a house, may require less grit than those where progress is hard to see, like teaching. It's also worth remembering that being gritty doesn't mean you never give up. It means using your passions to guide and prioritize your efforts, so you know when to persist and when to look for viable alternatives.

What can I try?

- **Draw A Grit Map:** Grab a sheet of paper and place it horizontally on a table. At the top, map the passions that give you a sense of purpose in your work and in your life. You might have one or two of these top-level goals that you want to stick with in the long-term. Below them, map the mid-level goals that make these passions possible. These are projects or activities that you really want to pour your energy into in order to achieve the things that matter to you most. Lastly, map your low-level goals. These are the day-to-day activities you need to complete to make all the other goals a reality. They are the means to an end. Giving up on lower-level goals sometimes is not only forgivable, but also absolutely necessary in order to stay on track. Put your grit map somewhere you can see it each day to keep you on track. Update your lower-level goals as needed so you can be gritty about the things that matter most.

- **Ask For Help:** Rely on other people to hold you accountable to your goals and help you persevere in the face of boredom, frustration, or discouragement. A common feature in the stories of top performers is that in those moments when they stumbled, doubted themselves, and wanted to quit, there was always someone close to them who encouraged them to persist.

- **Invest In Deliberate Practice:** Studies have found that people who become experts set clearly defined stretch goals that zero in on one narrow aspect of their overall performance. Then, with undivided attention and great effort, they strive to reach this goal. They regularly seek feedback on how they did and apply this feedback to their next effort. They repeat an action again and again and again until they've mastered what they set out to do and their conscious incompetence becomes unconscious competence. Then, they start all over again with a new stretch goal. While this kind of practice can be frustrating and exhausting, it can also be a positive and joyful experience as you see yourself improving over time.

Is there a habit I can play with?

When you set your priorities for the day (cue), make sure there's at least one opportunity to deliberately practice a skill that will advance you toward the goals you want to be most gritty about (routine). Then, celebrate by sharing or posting your challenge somewhere others can see it and offer you accountability and encouragement (reward).

Boosting Your Confidence

Do you ever wish you had more confidence? Does self-doubt hold you back from doing what you'd like? Researchers suggest that confidence is your ability to turn your thoughts into action. It's what allows you to start acting, risking, and failing, and to stop mumbling, apologizing, and hesitating. With it you can take on the world; without it, you remain stuck on the starting block of your own potential. This is why studies suggest that when it comes to your success at work, confidence matters more than competence. And while your genes, upbringing, and schooling have all been found to shape your levels of confidence, so do the choices you make each day. Your goal in building confidence shouldn't be to banish self-doubt, but to recognize when these uncomfortable feelings are warranted and avoid making the kind of mistakes associated with overconfidence, and when to move past them so they don't undermine your potential success or wellbeing.

How can I develop more confidence?

Researchers suggest that regularly turning your thoughts into action is the best way to build your confidence, especially when the action involves risk and failure. This means stepping outside your comfort zone, opening yourself up to learning, and discovering that sometimes failure provides your greatest lessons. Confidence can also be fueled by using your strengths in authentic ways, having the courage to share your vulnerabilities and imperfections, and being open to help from others.

What can I try?

- **Take One Small Step:** Acknowledging your self-doubt and taking small steps that lead to small wins can be an effective way to build your confidence and shift your beliefs about what you're capable of doing. What small step are you willing to try that can help you to grow and gain confidence? Write that step down, and then give it a try.

Record how it went. Then take another step. And another. Check back again from time to time and see where you started—the result just might surprise you!

- **Acknowledge "Not Yet":** Tune into the stories you tell yourself about what you can't do, what you've failed at, or why you're not good enough. Acknowledge that you can't do these things "yet," but recognize that with enough effort and learning, you can keep improving upon your abilities. When you hear yourself say "I can't," add on the word "yet." Let it remind you that you're on a learning curve.

- **Strike A Power Pose:** When you need a boost of confidence, find a private space and try a two-minute power pose. Stand like Wonder Woman or Superman (posture straight with your hands on your hips, feet in a wide stance, and head held high), and breathe slowly for two minutes. Notice how this leaves you feeling and then step forward with greater confidence.

Is there a habit I can play with?

When you brush your teeth (cue), nudge your body into an expanded pose of confidence by placing one hand on your hip and stand tall and open like Wonder Woman or Superman (routine). Then spit and rinse (reward).

Being Self-Compassionate

When things go wrong, what do you say to yourself in these moments? Do you chastise yourself with harsh words of self-criticism, or do you soothe yourself with kind words of self-compassion? Unfortunately, researchers have found that for many of us, self-criticism is our first response as our brain tries to protect us from making mistakes that may harm us. The problem with this approach is it can shift your brain into a state of self-inhibition and self-punishment that leaves you feeling threatened, demoralized, and often stuck in a cycle of rumination, procrastination, and self-loathing that makes it hard to take effective action. Studies suggest that tapping into your self-compassion, on the other hand, can help you to break your entrenched patterns of self-criticism while still allowing you to be honest about your fears. Triggering your brain's self-care and self-awareness systems helps you to see things in a more clear and balanced way, to remember that no one is perfect, and to enhance your motivation, performance, and resilience.

How can I develop more self-compassion?

Researchers suggest that there are three practices that can cultivate self-compassion. Firstly, being mindful and softening to the suffering or pain you might be experiencing, without overidentifying with your mistakes. Instead of labeling yourself as a "loser," "idiot," or "bad person," use touch—even just your hand placed on the opposite wrist or over your heart—and take some slow, deep breaths into the pain and acknowledge that you feel hurt and afraid and that's okay. Secondly, purposefully speak to yourself with kindness to soothe the pain, rather than reacting with judgement. It appears that using a soothing tone is as important as any words you say. Finally, accept that you are human and learning just like everybody else, rather than letting your expectations of perfection isolate you from others.

What can I try?

- **Create A Mantra:** A self-compassion mantra is a reminder to be kind to yourself. It makes it easier to soften and soothe, so that instead of your negative emotions hijacking your confidence, you can remain present, engaged, and authentic as you navigate your way through what's unfolding. What would a wise and kind friend say to you in the moments you want to beat yourself up? For example: "Hang on, in most situations you're better than you think you are. Let's figure this out." Or perhaps: "You've got this. Just slow down. Take a breath." Or even: "You're doing the best you can. Just be open to the learning and keep putting one foot in front of the other." How can you remind yourself to reach for this message in the moments when your inner-critic is firing up?

- **Write A Letter:** This can help you reflect when you are experiencing hurt or failure. Spend fifteen to twenty minutes writing a short letter to yourself about the situation. Think about what you would say to a friend in your position, or what a friend would say to you in this situation. Try to have understanding for your distress (e.g., "I am sad you feel distressed..."). Write whatever comes to you, but make sure it provides you with what you need to hear to feel nurtured and comforted about your stressful situation.

- **Soothe Your Pain:** Physical gestures can have an immediate effect on our bodies, activating the soothing parasympathetic nervous system. To get away from the stories in your head and drop into your body, try putting your hands over your heart, or simply place one hand over the top of the other in a comforting way when you need some self-compassion.

Is there a habit I can play with?

Remember To Be Kind. Wear a self-compassion bracelet to help you become aware of the harsh criticisms you give yourself. You can use any bracelet, or even a rubber band to do this. Every time you notice a self-criticism (cue), switch the bracelet to your other arm. Use the self-compassion mantra you've developed to acknowledge that this is a moment of suffering, that it is part of being human to experience difficulties, and to be kind to yourself (routine). Acknowledge your effort by gently holding the wrist that has the bracelet on to soothe yourself (reward).

Improving Your Resilience

When life throws you a curveball, how do you respond? Researchers have found that when you experience adversity or trauma, although it's painful, ninety percent of us have a psychological immune system that allows us to be naturally resilient and recover pretty quickly from these experiences. But the strength and speed of your response is often determined by the stories you tell yourself about why the adversity has occurred and what might happen next. In particular, studies suggest that themes of personalization (e.g., "It's all my fault"), pervasiveness (e.g., "I've ruined everything"), and permanence (e.g., "They will never get over this") within your stories impact the way you will think, feel, act, and recover from adversity. Studies have found that when you realize hardships are not entirely your fault, don't affect every aspect of your life, and won't follow you forever, that you are less likely to get depressed and are more able to solve problems, perform well at work, and cope with challenging people and situations.

That being said, self-care strategies will only go so far. In the case of severe trauma, it's important to draw on resources around you, such as family, friends, coworkers, your doctor, or professional help. When everything falls apart or you are placed under an excessive amount of stress for a long time, it wears you down, and it becomes important to take a break and get the help that you need to stay afloat.

How can I develop more resilience?

Many of the positive interventions in this book help build internal resources and strengths. By proactively building your internal resources over time, you will be better equipped to ride the storm and take care of yourself in the face of challenge. Researchers also suggest it can be helpful to tune into the stories you're telling yourself, particularly when you're feeling anxious, overwhelmed or upset, and notice the impact they're having on you. Ask yourself: "Is this story entirely accurate? Is it the only explanation for what's unfolding?" Then do a quick scan of the facts: Is it entirely your fault? Will it really affect everything? How long do you think the aftershocks will truly last? If it helps, studies have found we adapt to most things over time. Your goal should be to gently challenge your story with equally plausible facts or possibilities, not to delude yourself with fairy tales or unfounded optimism. As you review the alternative explanations you've created, choose to invest your attention and energy into the story that boosts your resilience and serves your wellbeing in this moment. Rinse and repeat as many times as needed.

What can I try?

- **Challenge Your Beliefs:** Write down a belief or story that's causing you anguish, then follow it with evidence or examples where the belief is false. For example: "I've completely embarrassed myself; I'll never be able to face these people again," could be countered with, "But chances are, they'll completely forget about it by tomorrow." As you allow yourself to sit with the fear and unease this story may hold, gently challenge the facts. Is this story true? Is it absolutely accurate? Have you over-personalized what happened or imagined it as more pervasive and permanent than it really might be? Is there another equally believable story that would be better to invest your energy and attention in until you know more?

- **Lean Into The Suck:** The experience of adversity is generally painful and unpleasant. Rather than adding more anxiety to these moments by trying to rid yourself of these feelings, lean into the "suck" and accept that what you're experiencing hurts and is upsetting. Don't be surprised or dismayed by these feelings. Know that they are part of your brain and body's natural protection and healing systems and instead of fighting them, denying them, or trying to rid yourself of them, let yourself experience the emotions and you will find they pass more quickly.

- **Ban "Always":** Words like "never" and "always" are signs of permanence mistakes in your thinking. No matter what happens to you at work or in life, nothing will *always* feel this awful. It will *sometimes* feel awful, and sometimes it won't. Likewise, it's not true that your work or your life will *never* be good again. It will *sometimes* not feel good, and sometimes it will. By becoming aware of the absolutes you tell in your stories, you can quickly regain a sense of control and choice.

- **Flex Your Stress Mindset:** What do you tell yourself and others about stress and challenge? Become aware of what you think and say when you experience stress or problems, and how you respond when others around you talk about their challenges. Is this mindset serving you well, or could you be more flexible in how you think about the potential benefits of challenge?

Is there a habit I can play with?

As you travel into work (cue), tune into the stories you're telling yourself about any challenges or adversities you may be facing at the moment. How are these stories causing you to think, feel, and act? If they're not serving you well, gently challenge them to see if there are other equally plausible explanations you may have missed and then invest your attention and energy into stories that boost your resilience and wellbeing (routine). Then get your morning coffee (reward).

CHAPTER 7

Heightening Health

"Every day you do one of two things: build health or produce disease in yourself." ~ Adelle Davis, American author

Let's face it—when you feel bad physically, it affects your energy levels, happiness, thoughts, behaviors, productivity, and relationships. Think of the last time that you had the flu. How did it make you feel? Probably pretty lousy. This is because your mind and body are closely interconnected.

Considerable research has focused on how to support good physical health. Many things influence your physical health, including your genes and biology, personality, financial resources, where you live, and the quality of your social relationships. Healthy behaviors, including eating well, moving often, restful sleep, and mindfully restoring yourself are foundational to maintaining good physical health. A growing number of studies are finding that these behaviors are critical not only to your physical health, but also support other aspects of your wellbeing, including your mental health, social relationships, and cognitive functioning.

Unfortunately, researchers suggest that we tend to be lousy judges of how much looking after our body impacts our performance and our wellbeing. We assume that one less hour of sleep to finish off that report or to catch up with friends won't make that much difference to how we'll feel in the morning. And indeed, getting a bit less sleep once in a while probably has little impact. The problem is that we do it repeatedly. We cheat ourselves of sleep a little at a time, creating a growing deficit which becomes more problematic with time. For example, one study found that losing ninety minutes of sleep is likely to reduce your daytime alertness by nearly one-third. And according to another researcher, four hours of sleep loss produced the same level of impairment as drinking a six-pack of beer before work.

And if you do sleep, is it restful? Our modern society makes it hard to shut off. Our rooms are filled with technology, and studies find that the glow from the electronic devices interrupts sleep patterns. As people take work home with them, it's hard to wind down. The result is that not only do we spend less time sleeping, the sleep we do get is often not restful.

When we sleep, we move through multiple cycles of REM (rapid eye movement), shallow, and deep sleep. It's the deep sleep stage where recovery and restoration really occurs. Think about your computer. If you keep it on for days on end, working with lots of programs, problems start to arise. It needs a reboot—shutting down completely, clearing things out, and starting again. The deep sleep stage is like rebooting your mind. But when you are sleep deprived, you spend most of your time in REM or shallow sleep, not reaching the restorative deep sleep stage. The effects of this build up cumulatively over time, ultimately affecting your energy levels, mental health, cognitive functioning, work performance, and physical health. "Like a drunk," Harvard sleep expert, Charles Czeisler, wrote, "a person who is sleep deprived has no idea how functionally impaired he or she truly is. Most of us have forgotten what it really feels like to be awake."

What and when we eat also affects how we feel and function. For example, foods like pasta, bread, cereal, and soda release glucose quickly, giving you a burst of energy, followed by a slump. Meanwhile, other foods, like high-fat meals (think cheeseburgers), can provide more sustained energy, but require your digestive system to work harder, reducing oxygen levels in your brain and making you groggy. Eating one huge meal makes your system work harder than smaller meals scattered through the day. The problem is that you're often at your lowest point in both energy and self-control by the time you try to decide what to eat, making a large burger and fries, or even a small chocolate brownie, hard to resist.

Our modern environments also make it a challenge to eat a healthy diet, even with good intentions. Unhealthy food options often seem easier and quicker to grab, causing you to think you're saving time without appreciating the impact on your performance thirty minutes later! It can be hard to manage your food choices when you attend poorly catered workshops or meetings, or when the healthy salmon dish you order at the restaurant arrives smothered in a high-sugar sauce. And if you're completely honest, sometimes no matter how bad you know a particular food or drink is for you, the taste is so good and triggers your brain's pleasure sensors, or the shared experience with friends so enjoyable, that you just don't care what you're putting into your body.

And then there's physical activity. We are made to move. Our bones and muscles need movement—without use, they atrophy, cells weaken, the body breaks down, ultimately resulting in frailty and illness. Unfortunately, if you have the belief that exercising three times a week should have you covered when it comes to getting enough movement, we hate to tell you that it is probably nowhere near enough to counter all the hours you spend sitting. Declared the most underrated health threat of our time, it turns out that on average, most of us sit for around nine hours a day. Yes, we spend more time sitting than sleeping. Just take a moment now to add it up: you were probably sitting while you had breakfast, traveled to work, attended a few meetings, sent some emails, had your lunch, made a few phone calls, completed key tasks, traveled home, ate your dinner, and watched some TV, or caught up with some friends. It all adds up. Frighteningly, researchers have found that inactivity is now killing more people than smoking, with some evidence that sitting for more than six hours a day greatly increases your risk of an early death. While movement keeps our metabolism up, keeping cholesterol in check, breaking down fat, and activating our muscles, sitting shuts these processes down. Over time, the effects accumulate, negatively impacting our health and wellbeing.

While a certain amount of sitting is helpful for resting and restoring energy, the problem is that it has become the dominant state that many of us find ourselves in. For most of us, sitting for most of the day is an inevitable part of our jobs. The key to countering this seems to be increasing our activity as much as possible by getting up and moving throughout the day. Every extra opportunity you take to move counts.

Movement also helps replenish and restore your energy. Many of us are constantly busy, filling our calendars with work, family, social events, and the list goes on and on. The feeling of being busy can be exhilarating—we feel alive and productive. But we focus on short-term feelings and gains, often at the expense of our long-term wellbeing. We need time to rest and restore, mentally and physically.

While this may all sound a little overwhelming, the good news is that researchers are finding that by making small, everyday changes to the way you sleep, eat, move, and restore yourself, you can create the kind of consistent thriving that you've been hoping for.

Michelle's Story: Learning To Eat Well

Born with a fast metabolism, I was able to spend most of my life eating mindlessly until I turned thirty and everything started to slow down. Challenged for the first time in my life to notice what I was consuming, I quickly realized there were a lot of stories I was invested in that made it hard to eat well.

For example, "My stomach doesn't wake up before lunch," turned out not to be true and I found I had far more energy and was more alert after two scrambled eggs for breakfast. Then there was, "I don't like the taste of whole grains," but it turned out that when the quality of the product is good, seed-based bread can be every bit as delicious as a white loaf. And, how about,

"I need sugar and fried foods for comfort," when low and behold, a bowl of fresh cherries or a handful of strawberries also works.

Despite my husband's self-righteousness (he'd been telling me for years that my stories about my body were flawed), as I began to slowly challenge my stories about food, I came to understand that what I ate did have a profound impact on my levels of energy. So now when it comes to eating, I consider what I have to do in the hours ahead and try to keep in reach quick, delicious, and good foods like protein balls, nuts, green smoothies, fresh fruit and vegetables, eggs, whole grain bread, and organic soups. In fact, these days even my husband admits that I generally eat better than he does.

It doesn't mean I don't still indulge in the odd glass of wine, spaghetti carbonara, or chocolate soufflé; it's just that I try to do so mindfully (and in small portions) at times when I don't need to rely heavily on my energy. Being mindful of what I eat has also helped me to notice the foods that feel good for me (like kale—who would have thought!), and the ones that don't serve me so well (unfortunately, custard donuts!). Far from being the burden I feared eating wisely might impose, it's actually given me the freedom to show up in life in the ways I value most (just don't tell my husband!).

Peggy's Story: The Limits Of Modern Medicine

As part of a four-month study-abroad program, I was living in Quito, Ecuador when a nearby volcano exploded and covered the city with ash. Deciding to escape to the country for a weekend, my friend and I stopped by a food cart for a snack and I made the terrible mistake of not washing the fruit that I bought. What was I thinking?

By the time we arrived back in Quito, I was sicker than I could ever remember being in my life. The next few days were completely miserable and when I finally saw the doctor, he diagnosed me as having picked up a parasite that was destroying me from the inside. This was the kind of news you really don't want to hear when you're living abroad in a developing country, far from your family and regular health care.

The doctor gave me some sort of medicine which alleviated my immediate symptoms, but left me far from healthy. By the time I returned to the United States, I was still suffering from chronic pain and nausea and at times was having trouble breathing. I remained in this state of ill health for several years while I visited numerous doctors and had all sorts of tests done, but came no closer to understanding what the parasite was or what medicine I had been given in Ecuador. It was a pretty depressing time.

Eventually, I moved to California to begin graduate school and finally, completely disillusioned by the hope of modern medicine, I started to make small behavioral changes to try and improve my health. I discovered I had an egg allergy and became a vegetarian to try and simplify my diet. I started running and found that regular exercise helped me to feel physically and mentally better.

These days I can comfortably keep the pain and nausea at bay, provided I consistently eat well and move regularly. In the end, my small, daily health behaviors solved the problems that modern medicine had failed to fix and fueled my passion to study health psychology, mind-body connections, and what it means to thrive.

Heightening Health Toolkit

Sleeping Well	Forgo Sleep Ins	Create Bedtime Routines	Toss The Turning	
Eating Wisely	Plan Your Diet	Eat Small Meals Frequently	Track And Adjust	Savor Your Food
Moving Regularly	Count Your Steps	Get Up Regularly	Start Early	Move At Home
Mindfully Restore	Just Be	Mindfully Meditate	Create A Third Space	Mindful Breaks

Sleeping Well

How much sleep do you get each night? Researchers suggest that on average, ninety-five percent of us need somewhere between seven and nine hours of sleep per night. There are exceptions—some people need less sleep, others need more. But unfortunately, roughly two-thirds of us report that we don't get enough sleep and as a result, studies suggest we're damaging our health, our moods, our cognitive capacities, and our productivity.

Studies suggest that your body will run best on a twenty-four-hour schedule, following your natural circadian rhythm which regulates your sleeping, waking and energy cycles, but alterations to this cycle increase risk for fatigue over time. If you lose access to normal time cues (like daylight and darkness due to shift work, LED lights or technology that keeps you awake at all hours), it appears your body shifts into twenty-five-hour days, throwing off your sleep cycle by up to ten hours a week. This disruption of your natural rhythm has been found to contribute to a host of issues, from weight gain to heart problems and depression. While at first glance, this might seem like a problem for shift workers, travelers, and others with altered schedules, our modern lifestyles add additional disruptions.

How can I get more sleep?

Researchers suggest that one way to ensure you're getting enough sleep is to establish a bedtime routine that allows you to wind your mind down and get ready for sleep. Several hours before bedtime, turn off electronics, dim the lights, and slow down your routine. Ideally, this should happen at around the same time each night, to help maintain your body's natural sleeping and waking patterns. Additionally, studies have found that exposure to the light found in most electronic devices like TVs and smartphones in the hours before you go to sleep suppresses melatonin levels, making it harder to fall asleep, decreasing sleep quality, and even increasing the risk of high blood pressure and diabetes. Try turning technology off long before it's time to go to sleep and make your bedroom a place of rest. And while medications can be useful in the short-term, they should be used with caution as they can be highly addictive and make it more difficult to sleep in the long run.

What can I try?

- **Forgo Sleep Ins:** Try to maintain a consistent schedule of sleeping and waking, even on the weekend. Resist the urge to sleep in until noon. Instead, treat yourself to a one hour or less afternoon nap. At night, set an alarm to tell you it's time to get ready for bed. Keep in mind that your body has a tendency to push later and later if given the chance, so you need to get to bed before you hit your second wind.

- **Create Bedtime Routines:** Give yourself at least forty-five minutes to wind down before bed with clear nighttime cues to help your body relax. Dim the lights. Lower the temperature by two to four degrees. Turn off electronics (smartphones, iPads, computers, and TVs, or anything with blue LED light as it impacts your sleep hormones). Write down what's on your mind—especially unfinished to-dos or issues. Try some restorative yoga or meditate. Read a non-stimulating but enjoyable book. And get into bed at a decent time.

- **Toss The Turning:** Don't worry if you wake in the middle of the night. It appears that waking in the middle of the night is perfectly natural, given we've evolved to have what researchers call segregated sleeping—a first sleep and second sleep with a short waking period in between. Rather than lying there anxiously watching the minutes tick by, try some slow breathing or meditation. If you need to sit up for twenty minutes, keep the lights low and read or listen to some relaxing music before heading back to sleep. Even if you are not sleeping, quietly resting is beneficial. Studies have found this time can be the most relaxing time of your day, provided you're not worried about sleeping!

Is there a habit I can play with?

Set an alarm to start your bedtime routine each night (cue), and wind down in whatever way feels relaxing and restorative for you (routine). Then get into bed, breathe deeply and get a good night's rest (reward).

Eating Wisely

Is the food you're eating serving you well? While there's a lot of conflicting advice about what we should and shouldn't be eating and drinking, it's clear that no one advocates that you should intentionally consume more refined sugars, fried foods, or alcohol. Researchers suggest that it may be helpful to start thinking about food not as calories, but as energy. After all, just about everything you eat is converted by your body into glucose, which provides the energy your body and brain need to stay alert and productive. When you're running low on glucose, you have a tough time staying focused, your attention drifts and your body becomes sluggish—which helps to explain why it's hard to do anything very productive on an empty stomach. Studies have found that eating well not only bolsters your health in the short- and long-term, but it can also improve your physical appearance and mood, and keep your energy levels high.

How can I eat more wisely?

Researchers suggest that the trick to eating right is not learning to resist temptation. It's making healthy eating the easiest possible option. Plan your diet, make food ahead of time, and make healthy options readily available. Remember that when you choose foods with less fat (but with some healthy fats), fewer carbs (you still need some), little added sugar (aim for unprocessed sugars, like fruit), and more protein, you'll feel healthier. In particular, eating up to seven servings of fruit and vegetables—especially those green in color—has been found to relate to health and happiness. Avoid crazy diets that rely on a single food or drink. Above all, incorporate moderation throughout your diet. Too much of anything is harmful and the occasional indulgence in unhealthy foods is fine in small amounts—the key is finding the right balance that makes you feel healthy and strong.

What can I try?

- **Plan Your Diet:** Make your eating decisions before you get hungry. Studies show that you'll do a lot better at resisting salt, calories, and unhealthy fats in the future than in the present moment. Think about the meals and snacks you will have access to and be able to control this week. What can you have on hand to make good eating choices easier? Try to set your sights on foods that are good for your short-term energy and long-term health.

- **Eat Small Meals Frequently:** The body's metabolism is meant to process energy on a regular basis. Spikes and drops in blood sugar are bad for your productivity, your brain, and your body. Smaller, more frequent meals maintain your glucose at a more consistent level than relying on a midday meal or big evening feast. Start your day right with a high-protein breakfast, then note where your natural energy slumps occur during the day (for many of us it's around ten a.m., one p.m., four p.m., and seven p.m.). At these times, stop to eat something nourishing and reflect on your water consumption (we often mistake thirst for hunger).

- **Track And Adjust:** There are a few good and a few bad ingredients in most meals. No matter how hard you try, you will eat some foods that are not ideal. So do a little accounting in your head, on a piece of paper, or with an app so you can keep track of what you consume. Ask yourself if what you are about to eat is a net gain or a net loss for your energy, based on what you know about all the ingredients. Look for foods with less fat, fewer carbohydrates, and as little added sugar and preservatives as possible. Look out for a long list of ingredients that you've never heard of. Then, keep servings small and indulgences rare (pick the moments you can afford the energy slumps), and you're likely to have less guilt, more enjoyment, and better health. By developing the habit of asking this question, you will make better decisions in the moment and be aware of how you're tracking across the day.

Is there a habit I can play with?

When it's time for lunch (cue), get up from your desk. If you can, go outside and sit where there is greenery and eat your meal mindfully. If not, pick a quiet location that lets you focus on your meal. Leave work behind. Try to choose foods for your lunch that will replenish your energy (routine). After you **Savor Your Food**, put on a favorite song and kick back to some great music for a few minutes (reward).

Moving Regularly

Roughly how many minutes do you spend moving your body each week? Researchers suggest that while thirty minutes of physical activity, five times a week, seems to be a good guide for most of us, exercise alone is not enough. Being active throughout the day is what will keep you healthy and offset the chronic inactivity most of us experience in our days. Why bother? Studies suggest that regular physical activity and exercise helps prevent and manage physical illness, including heart disease, diabetes, lung disease, and certain types of cancer, and lowers the risk of death. It can also improve the way the brain works because exercise spurs the release of soothing neurotransmitters, including serotonin, norepinephrine, and dopamine, and increases levels of brain chemicals called growth factors. These help make new brain cells and establish new connections between brain cells to help you learn and improve your memory and attention. Regular exercise has also been found to be one of the best ways to ensure you get a good night's sleep, improve your mood, reduce your risk of mental illness, and function better.

How can I move more?

Studies have found that there are hundreds of moments in a typical day where you can embed extra activity in your routine. Current recommmendations are that you need at least 150 minutes of moderate physical activity (the kind that increases your heart rate) each week. It's also beneficial to include activities to build strength and stay flexible. This doesn't mean you have to hit the gym or head out for a run, but simply that you stay active. You can increase your heart rate by walking briskly, gardening, doing housework, and swimming, and build your strength and flexibility with yard work, lifting children, and activities like yoga and Pilates. The key is to find activities that you enjoy doing and are willing to do on a regular basis. Check with a doctor or health expert for the amount and types of exercise that are best for your body and to figure out the kinds of exercise you enjoy doing and are most likely to stick with. After all, even a little bit of exercise that you actually do is better than no exercise at all.

What can I try?

- **Count Your Steps:** Get a Fitbit or download a free app to your smartphone to start measuring the number of steps you take each day. Start small—aim for 5,000 steps, and work your way up to 10,000 steps per day (if you're doing other forms of exercise, most apps have ways to convert it into steps). Upload your report and track your steps online, which can show you your progress over time, and how you compare to others. Don't beat yourself up if you miss the goal—some days will be easier to get steps in than others; instead, think about how you can add a few more steps tomorrow.

- **Get Up Regularly:** When you have no choice but to sit for several hours a day, at least break it up. Set a timer that goes off every twenty to thirty minutes. Walk around the office and drink a glass of water—this gets you moving, keeps you hydrated, and if you spend a lot of time staring at a computer, helps your eyesight. Taking regular movement breaks can improve your creativity and productivity—helping you work smarter, not longer. If you sit through meetings all day, stand in the back of the room for part of the time.

- **Start Early:** Just twenty minutes of moderate activity could significantly improve your mood for the next twelve hours. So, while working out in the evening is better than no activity at all, you essentially sleep through and miss most of the boost to your mood. Exercising at the beginning of the day kick-starts your metabolism, helping you burn additional fat and improve your glucose tolerance. As the day wears on, it's also easier to create more excuses. Begin your day with a brisk walk, a stop at the local gym, or a twenty-minute yoga session at home.

- **Move At Home:** A study of more than 6,000 people who had successfully kept weight off revealed that the most effective and sustainable changes start in the home. Ninety-two percent of the participants in this study found a way to exercise at home. Whether you use a treadmill, a set of handheld weights, online aerobic programs, exercise in your neighborhood, or being active with your children, your home is a great place to build an active lifestyle.

Is there a habit I can play with?

When you are talking on the phone (cue), stand up rather than remaining sitting at your desk (routine). Add these minutes to your daily movement tally so you can see how much extra movement you're getting (reward).

Mindfully Restore

What have you done in the last week to slow down and mindfully restore your energy? If you're like most of the people we meet, it will be a very short list! Yet, researchers have found that when you expend too much energy without sufficient recovery periods, eventually your body will burnout and break down. Your body is not a machine that works away at a steady, unrelenting rhythm. Instead, like every other part of nature, it pulses in rhythm patterns that ebb and flow. Your energy is a finite resource. For example, studies suggest that during your waking hours, you experience an ultradian rhythm that, in ninety to 120-minute cycles, craves a period of rest and recovery before your energy is restored. Often signalled by physical restlessness, yawning, hunger, procrastination, difficulty concentrating, or increasing tension, these natural cycles can be overridden to draw on your energy reserves, but doing so releases more cortisol into your body which over time prompts symptoms such as hyperactivity, aggressiveness, impatience, irritability, anger, self-absorption, and insensitivity to others. This increases the risk for a host of physical and mental illnesses, including early mortality.

How can I mindfully restore?

Researchers suggest that breaking your day into a series of manageable intervals consistent with your own physiological needs and ultradian rhythm (your ninety- to 120-minute cycle), punctuated by regular recovery breaks, is the key to peak performance. The length of renewal is less important than the quality. It is possible to get a great deal of recovery in a few minutes if it involves a ritual that allows you to disengage from work and truly recharge. This could range from getting up to talk to a colleague about something other than work, listening to a favorite song, watching a funny cat video, or walking up and down the stairs.

It is also important to recognize and value the importance of rest. As the boundaries between work and nonwork life increasingly blur, it becomes harder to switch off and evenings and weekends turn into work time. Set boundaries around when and where you are willing to work. Take time out each week for other activities, including spending time with family and friends, exercise, and hobbies that you enjoy. Give yourself permission to not work. By mindfully and regularly restoring your energy, you'll be more motivated, focused, and productive in your work, and in the long-term, feel better overall.

What can I try?

- **Just Be:** Take small moments in your day to just breathe and be. Try a box breathing technique by closing your mouth and breathing in slowly through your nose. Count to four as you inhale. Hold your breath for four seconds. You are not trying to deprive your body of oxygen, but need to allow a few seconds for the air to fill your lungs. Concentrate on your belly and notice how it also moves when you inhale deeply. Open your mouth slightly and slowly exhale to a count of four. Hold the exhale for another count of four. Ideally, you should repeat the exercise for four minutes, but two or three times will help you to achieve a more relaxed state, relieve tension, and settle your nerves.

- **Mindfully Meditate:** Begin for just two minutes. Sit quietly and set an intention for your meditation—it might be to improve your wellbeing, to restore yourself, or to practice training your mind—and once you're clear on why you're sitting in stillness, simply bring your attention gently to your breath. You may find yourself in a state where your mind is calm and concentrated and this may last for a long time, or for just a few seconds. If you find yourself getting distracted and realize your attention has wandered, rather than beating yourself up, just practice bringing your wandering attention back to focus on your breath. Acknowledge that you're learning, remind yourself of your intention, and this time try to stay focused a little longer on your breath. Over time, as your ability to focus your attention improves, keep extending the time for as long as you can. Even two to five minutes of meditation, twice a day, can lead to profound changes in your mindset, your levels of calm, and your restoration.

- **Create A Third Space:** The "third space" refers to the space between one activity (the first space of what you've just done) and another (the second space of what you're about to do). It is the time you spend in transition and offers a mini-moment for recovery throughout your day. During this transition period, take a few minutes to reflect on what went well and what you've learned, to take a few deep breaths, and to have a little rest and set your intentions for the next actions you're about to take.

Is there a habit I can play with?

Take **Mindful Breaks**. When you feel your energy waning (cue), take a few minutes to rest and recover by getting up and stretching, filling your glass with water, and setting your intention for the next sprint of activity (routine). Set your alarm to go off in ninety or 120 minutes so you can take your next recovery break (reward).

Maintaining Your Wellbeing

So how does this all come together to help you feel and function better at work and in life? A blueprint is used in architecture to provide a vision of what will be created, and a specific plan of action for the builders, designers, supervisors, and others involved in the project. It is built upon a strong knowledge base—the best of what is known for developing a sound structure, with adjustments made to fit the desires and needs of the customer and designer and the conditions in which the structure will reside. It is a work in progress, continually being updated by current knowledge.

Throughout this book, we have tried to provide you with a vision of what might be possible for your own wellbeing blueprint. We've offered you evidence-based tools for developing a sound structure, urged you to make adjustments as you desire, and encouraged you to build in feedback loops to ensure your efforts are delivering the outcomes you most want and so that your blueprint can be updated and refined. Remember, your goal is to become an intelligent and empowered steward of your own wellbeing.

In helping you to create your blueprint, we have focused primarily on the factors that you have more control over—how you think and feel, your response to different events, and how you interact with other people. But a blueprint is only useful if it becomes the basis for action. If it's not carried forward, then it is simply lines on a piece of paper that never materialize.

We find that the most common reason people struggle with their wellbeing is that they're "too busy" to find the time to start feeling good and functioning more effectively. And while we completely understand the reality of living busy lives, doesn't not prioritizing a few minutes every day to look after your wellbeing seem a little crazy? After all, the evidence you've seen throughout this book repeatedly suggests that the impact these activities will have on your performance, your energy levels, and your health offers some significant payoffs.

We believe that just as you might want to ban the words "always" and "never" to improve your resilience (see Chapter 6), the same is true of the words "too busy." The truth is, no matter how many people are demanding our time (and in our lives this includes bosses, clients, colleagues, family and pets), to a large extent we are each busy with what we've chosen to say "yes" to. As hard as this may be to initially accept, the goods news is that it means you can prioritize even just a few minutes a day to look after your wellbeing, if you choose to. And if you find it hard to believe you are worth the time to look after yourself, then start by doing it so that you have the energy to look after all the other people who are relying on you.

Of course, just because a blueprint is well designed, it doesn't mean the building always goes as planned. You are human and that means you will make mistakes along the way, bump up against your limitations, and suffer set backs from time to time. Some weeks—and possibly some months— your wellbeing activities will go perfectly to plan and you'll truly feel like you're thriving. At other times, it might feel like your best efforts have come completely undone, the practices you've chosen are simply not working, or you'll realize that you've sabotaged yourself and will feel like you're completely struggling. And in all of these moments it's important to remember that maintaining our wellbeing is a fluid experience of highs and lows for every one of us, a journey of learning rather than a final destination. Simply keep coming back to your blueprint as needed, note what's working well and what's not, then make any adjustments and try again.

You will also find there are things that impact your wellbeing that are beyond the control of your blueprint. There are the big things that really shake your world, and the smaller uncontrollable factors that are often invisible to anyone but you. There are things that might be happening in your home—a troubled spouse, a child having problems at school, or an elderly parent for whom you're caring. And the things happening around you at work—jobs being reorganized, workforces being downsized and bosses who seem to always demand more. These are the broader system factors that also impact your wellbeing.

Changing a whole system of any kind can be challenging, but as anthropologist Margaret Mead famously noted: "Never doubt that a small group of thoughtful, committed citizens can change the world; indeed, it's the only thing that ever has." In fact, researchers have found that much of your behavior is contagious; that your habits, attitudes and actions spread through a complicated web of connections to infect those around you. For example, one study found that your happiness can trigger a chain reaction that benefits not only your friends, your friends' friends, and their friends' friends' friends for up to a year (although this can be limited by geographical distance). And while sadness also spreads through your networks, it is not as robust as happiness.

This means that looking after your own wellbeing is a good and necessary step. Far from being selfish or pointless, when you are feeling good and functioning effectively—like a single butterfly flapping its wings and creating a hurricane halfway around the world—your small changes can trigger a cascade of positive ripples through your organization, your family, and your community.

As you develop your blueprint and become a more informed and empowered steward of your wellbeing, you can pay forward what you've discovered and intentionally help others to also feel good and function more effectively. If you're a leader in your organization, you can use many of the ideas from this book to improve the wellbeing of your team (this is how Michelle started—you can find more examples of team activities at **www.michelle mcquaid.com**). You can share the activities you're practicing around the dinner table with your family and take on different wellbeing challenges together. You can offer to talk about what you're learning in your community—you don't need to be a positive psychology expert, just be honest about what you're learning and open up the space for others to do the same.

So what does your wellbeing blueprint look like? What do you need to do to take control of your wellbeing and take hold of the life you want to be living? Thriving begins with a single step. We wish you well with your journey, wherever it may lead you.

"My mission in life is not merely to survive,
but to thrive; and to do so with some passion, some compassion,
some humor and some style." ~ Maya Angelou

Acknowledgements

With heartfelt thanks...

Our journey to write this book has been as rich as the content in it, and there have been many wonderful people who have contributed with their presence, love, and expertise.

Thank you to all of the amazing organizations and people in them who, like us, believe that the future of our world depends on more people being able to consistently thrive at work. Thank you for trusting us to help guide you through our workshops, coaching, classes, and programs. Thank you for allowing us to measure the impact of our collective efforts so we can continue to improve our practices. We are extremely proud of what we are achieving together.

Thank you to the MAPP communities and wellbeing coaches and practitioners around the globe who extend the reach of these insights and practices into countries, workplaces, and homes that we could never dream of reaching. To hear how you are sharing these ideas from the Bahamas to Oman, and so many countries in between, is an incredible privilege, and we feel honored to help in any small way to aid the important difference you're making for yourself, your families, your friends, your workplaces, and communities. This book would not exist without your courage, generosity, and inspiration.

This book and our work would not be possible without the ongoing research of remarkable leaders, especially in the fields of social science, positive psychology and neuroscience. We want to give special thanks to Professor Martin Seligman for his vision of a world where more people consistently flourish and his generosity in sharing his wellbeing framework for others to measure and build upon. Our heartfelt thanks goes to the researchers whose tireless efforts help to make each of the PERMAH pillars more tangible and practical, including Barbara Fredrickson, Mihaly Csikszentmihalyi, Chris Peterson, the VIA Institute, Jane Dutton, Christine Porath, Michael Steger, Emily Esfhani Smith, Robert Vallerand, Carol Dweck, Kristen Neff, Angela Duckworth, Sonja Lyubormirsky, Howard Friedman, George Vaillant, Ed Diener, Felicia Huppert, Paul Wong, Carol Ryff, Kim Cameron, Tom Rath, Lea Waters, Scott Barry Kaufman, and so many others. Please keep leading us forward.

From Michelle

To my team, thank you for supporting my big dreams. Every word of this book was lovingly poured over by Debbie Hindle and Rachel Taylor, who challenge my thinking every day. The design of this book is a reflection of the creativity and persistence of Caitlin Judd. The printing of this book is a testament to the organizational and loving ass-kicking skills of Rachel Caradine. Your ability to take the PERMAH Workplace Survey online is a result of the technological prowess and self-compassion of Michelle Millichip and her team. And the fact that you even found this book is the result of the unwavering passion of Michelle Etheve, who shares all our work with the world. You guys fill my world with joy and possibility.

And to my family, Patrick, Charlie, and Jamie, thank you for helping me to keep my passion harmonious and reminding me that the best way to improve my wellbeing is a hug, a bad joke, or a tickle fight at least once a day. You are what makes my life worth living.

From Peggy

To those who have been my encouragement and support through the years—thank you for believing in me, even as I have doubted myself. To my mom and in memory of my dad—thank you for being there for me through the highs and lows of my life, always there as my encouragement and support. I would not be where I am today without you there beside me.

To those in academia who have guided and mentored me in my journey—especially Professors Howard Friedman and Leslie Martin. Thank you for taking me on board and teaching me in so many ways.

Thank you to Julie Butler, for her work in developing the foundations for measuring wellbeing, and to all of the students that I have had the opportunity to work with over the years. You continually challenge me to consider how my research studies translate into real world contexts. Thank you for inspiring me to move beyond the safety of academia to try and make a real impact on the world.

And in honor of Dr. Christine Siokou, my colleague and friend. You left this world far too early. I was truly blessed by the time that I had with you. You changed my worldview completely, and I'm a better person for the time I was privileged to spend with you. Your spirit lives on through each of us who have been deeply touched by your life.

References

Chapter 1. Thriving in Life = Feeling Good + Functioning Well

In its simplest form, wellbeing is your ability to feel good and function effectively...
Huppert, F. A. & So, T. T. (2013). Flourishing Across Europe: Application of a New Conceptual Framework for Defining Well-being. *Social Indicators Research, 110(3)*, 837-861.

Studies are finding that high levels of wellbeing relate to all sorts of positive outcomes... Lyubomirsky, S., King, L. A., & Diener, E. (2005). The Benefits of Frequent Positive Affect. *Psychological Bulletin, 131*, 803-855.

A recent study shows that when it comes to our wellbeing, seventy per cent of us... Rath, T. & Harter, J. K. (2010). *Wellbeing: The five essential pillars.* Gallup Press.

In 1998, Professor Martin Seligman, who was the president of the American Psychological Association... Seligman, M. E. & Csikszentmihalyi, M. (2000). *Positive psychology: An introduction* (Vol. 55, No. 1, p. 5). American Psychological Association.

More than 18,000 peer-reviewed research articles... Rusk, R. D. & Waters, L. E. (2013). Tracing the size, reach, impact, and breadth of positive psychology. *The Journal of Positive Psychology, 8(3)*, 207-221.

Researchers have proposed numerous theories of what wellbeing... Ryff, C. D. & Keyes, C. L. M. (1995). The Structure of Psychological Well-being Revisited. *Journal of Personality and Social Psychology, 69(4)*, 719; Huppert, F. A. (2008). Mental capital and well-being: making the most of ourselves in the 21st century. *State-of-science review. Psychological Wellbeing: Evidence Regarding its Causes and Consequences. SR-X2.* London: Government Office for Science Foresight project.

In 2011, Professor Seligman suggested his own model... Seligman, M. E. (2011). *Flourish: A Visionary New Understanding of Happiness and Well-being.* New York, NY: Simon and Schuster.

We (and many others) believe that physical health is also a key part of wellbeing... Rath, T. (2013). *Eat Move Sleep: How Small Choices Lead to Big Changes.* New York, NY: Missionday.

Positive interventions are simple activities that can help you feel good and function well... Lyubomirsky, S. & Layous, K. (2013). How Do Simple Positive Activities Increase Well-being? *Current Directions in Psychological Science, 22*(1), 57-62.

Researchers believe that your wellbeing—much like your body weight—has a genetically determined set-point range... Diener, E. & Biswas-Diener, R. (2011). *Happiness: Unlocking the Mysteries of Psychological Wealth.* New York, NY: John Wiley & Sons.

Feedback loops are invisible forces that help shape human behavior... Heath, C. & Heath, D. (2011). *Switch: How to change things when change is hard.* Waterville, Me: Thorndike Press.

Through a series of studies, they whittled the items down to twenty-three questions... Butler, J. & Kern, M. L. (2016). The PERMA-Profiler: A brief multidimensional measure of flourishing. *International Journal of Wellbeing, 6*(3).

Peggy subsequently created an alternative measure, which was specifically designed to measure wellbeing at work... Kern, M. L., Waters, L., Adler, A. & White, M. (2014). Assessing employee wellbeing in schools using a multifaceted approach: Associations with physical health, life satisfaction, and professional thriving. *Psychology, 5*(6), 500.

Researchers have discovered that while eighty-nine percent of us believe that tomorrow will be better than today... Lopez, S. J. (2013). *Making Hope Happen: Create the Future You Want for Yourself and Others.* New York, NY: Simon and Schuster.

By focusing on small, achievable goals, you can see change occur and build confidence and momentum along the way... Heath, C. & Heath, D. (2011). *Switch: How to Change Things When Change Is Hard.* Waterville, Me: Thorndike Press.

Habitual behavior is driven in part by reward loops in our brains, which include cues, routines, and rewards... Graybiel, A. M. (1998). The basal ganglia and chunking of action repertoires. *Neurobiology of learning and memory, 70*(1), 119-136.

The human brain excels at adapting to our conditions... Lyubomirsky, S. (2014). *The Myths of Happiness: What Should Make You Happy, but Doesn't, What Shouldn't Make You Happy, but Does.* New York, NY: Penguin.

Chapter 2: Promoting Positive Emotions

Researchers have found that the experience of heartfelt positive emotions... Green, S., McQuaid, M., Putell, A. & Dulagil, A. (in press). The Psychology of Positivity at Work. In Oades, L.G., Steger, M., Delle-Fave, A. & Passmore, J. (Eds.). *The Wiley-Blackwell Handbook of the Psychology of Positivity and Strengths-Based Approaches at Work.* Chichester, UK: Wiley-Blackwell.

Studies conducted by Professor Barbara Fredrickson from the University of North Carolina have repeatedly demonstrated... Fredrickson, B. L. (2013). Positive Emotions Broaden and Build. In E. Ashby Plant & P. G. Devine (Eds.). *Advances in Experimental Social Psychology* (Vol. 47, pp. 1–53). Burlington, VT: Academic Press.

Studies have found that when you are in in a positive mood, your field of peripheral vision expands... Wadlinger, H. A. & Isaacowitz, D. M. (2006). Positive mood broadens visual attention to positive stimuli. *Motivation and Emotion, 30*(1), 87–99; Rowe, G., Hirsh, J. B. & Anderson, A. K. (2007). Positive affect increases the breadth of attentional selection. *Proceedings of the National Academy of Sciences of the United States of America, 104*, 383–388; Schmitz, T. W., De Rosa, E. & Anderson, A. K. (2009). Opposing influences of affective state valence on visual cortical encoding. *The Journal of Neuroscience, 29*(22), 7199–7207; Trick, L. M., Brandigampola, S. & Enns, J. T. (2012). How fleeting emotions affect hazard perception and steering while driving: The impact of image arousal and valence. *Accident Analysis and Prevention, 45, 222.*

Think more quickly and creatively, by flooding your brain with the neurotransmitters dopamine and serotonin... Fredrickson, B. L. & Branigan, C. (2005). Positive emotions broaden the scope of attention and thought-action repertoires. *Cognition and Emotion, 19*(3), 313–332.

Connect better and attune to others... Fredrickson, B.L. (2009). *Positivity: Groundbreaking Research Reveals How to Embrace the Hidden Strength of Positive Emotions, Overcome Negativity, and Thrive.* New York, NY: Random House; Dunn, J. R. & Schweitzer, M. E. (2005). Feeling and Believing: The Influence of Emotion on Trust. *Journal of Personality and Social Psychology, 88*(5), 736–748; Dovidio, J. F., Isen, A. M., Guerra, P., Gaertner, S. L. & Rust, M. (1998). Positive affect, cognition, and the reduction of intergroup bias. In C. Sedikides (Ed.), *Intergroup cognition and intergroup behavior* (pp. 337–366). Mahwah, NJ: Erlbaum; Johnson, K. J. & Fredrickson, B. L. (2005). "We all look the same to me": Positive emotions eliminate the own-race in face recognition. *Psychological Science, 16*(11), 875–881.

As positive emotions accrue they help to build... Aspinwall, L. G. (2001). Dealing with Adversity: Self-regulation, Coping, Adaptation, and Health. In A. Tesser & N. Schwarz (Eds.), *The Blackwell Handbook of Social Psychology: Vol. 1.* Intraindividual processes (pp. 591–614). Malden, MA: Blackwell; Fredrickson, B. L. (1998). What Good Are Positive Emotions? *Review of General Psychology,* 2, 300–319; Fredrickson, B. L. & Joiner, T. (2002). Positive Emotions Trigger Upward Spirals Toward Emotional Wellbeing. *Psychological Science,* 13(2), 172–175; Isen, A. M. (1990). The influence of positive and negative affect on cognitive organization: Some implications for development. In N. Stein, B. Leventhal, & T. Trabasso (Eds.), *Psychological and Biological Approaches to Emotion* (pp. 75–94). Hillsdale, NJ: Erlbaum.

The right amount of anxiety... Kashdan, T. & Biswas-Diener, R. (2014). *The Upside of Your Dark Side: Why Being Your Whole Self—Not Just Your "Good" Self—Drives Success and Fulfillment.* New York, NY: Penguin.

Fredrickson's research does suggest that it can be helpful to find the right balance... Fredrickson, B. L. (2013b). Updated Thinking on Positivity Ratios. *American Psychologist, 68,* 814-822.

Experiencing heartfelt positive emotions creates an upward spiral... Fredrickson, B. L. & Joiner, T. (2002). Positive Emotions Trigger Upward Spirals Toward Emotional Wellbeing. *Psychological Science, 13*(2), 172–175.

You can't create genuine heartfelt positive emotions by just trying to think happy thoughts... Fredrickson, B.L. (2009). *Positivity: Groundbreaking Research Reveals How to Embrace the Hidden Strength of Positive Emotions, Overcome Negativity, and Thrive.* New York, NY: Random House.

Jolts of Joy... Garland, E. L., Fredrickson, B., Kring, A. M., Johnson, D. P., Meyer, P. S. & Penn, D. L. (2010). Upward spirals of positive emotions counter downward spirals of negativity: Insights from the broaden-and-build theory and affective neuroscience on the treatment of emotion dysfunctions and deficits in psychopathology. *Clinical Psychology Review,* 30(7), 849-864.

Hunt And Gather... Fredrickson, B.L. (2009). Positivity: Groundbreaking Research Reveals How to Embrace the Hidden Strength of Positive Emotions, Overcome Negativity, and Thrive. New York, NY: Random House.

Connect with Nature... Kaplan, S. (1995). The restorative benefits of nature: Toward an integrative framework. *Journal of Environmental Psychology, 15*(3), 169-182.

Studies suggest that while ruminating like this might feel like a way of working things out... Fredrickson, B.L. (2009). Positivity: Groundbreaking Research Reveals How to Embrace the Hidden Strength of Positive Emotions, Overcome Negativity, and Thrive. New York, NY: Random House.

Try not to prolong bad feelings beyond the insight and growth they have provided... McQuaid, M. (2017). Is Positive Psychology Still Relevant in 2017? *Huffington Post,* retrieved from http://www.huffingtonpost.com/michelle-mcquaid/is-positive-psychology-st_1_b_14565078.html

Create Healthy Distractions... Fredrickson, B.L. (2009). *Positivity: Groundbreaking Research Reveals How to Embrace the Hidden Strength of Positive Emotions, Overcome Negativity, and Thrive.* New York, NY: Random House.

Disrupt Negative Thoughts... Fredrickson, B.L. (2009). *Positivity: Groundbreaking Research Reveals How to Embrace the Hidden Strength of Positive Emotions, Overcome Negativity, and Thrive.* New York, NY: Random House.

Navigate Negativity Landmines... Fredrickson, B.L. (2009). *Positivity: Groundbreaking Research Reveals How to Embrace the Hidden Strength of Positive Emotions, Overcome Negativity, and Thrive.* New York, NY: Random House.

Limit Media Time... Fredrickson, B.L. (2009). *Positivity: Groundbreaking Research Reveals How to Embrace the Hidden Strength of Positive Emotions, Overcome Negativity, and Thrive.* New York, NY: Random House.

Worry Time... Frish, M.B. (2006). *Quality of Life Therapy.* New Jersey: Wiley & Sons.

Studies suggest that kind people experience more happiness and gratitude... Otake, K., Shimai, S., Tanaka-Matsumi, J., Otsui, K. & Fredrickson, B. L. (2006). Happy people become happier through kindness: A counting kindnesses intervention. *Journal of Happiness Studies, 7,* 361–375; Gander, F., Proyer, R.T., Ruch, W. & Wyss, T. (2013). Strength-based Positive Interventions: Further evidence for their potential in enhancing well-being and alleviating depression. *Journal of Happiness Studies, 12,* 1241-1259.

kindness is contagious... Fowler, J. H. & Christakis, N. A. (2010). Cooperative behavior cascades in human social networks. *Proceedings of the National Academy of Sciences, 107*(12), 5334-5338.

Researchers have argued that kindness is like a muscle... Pavey, L., Greitemeyer, T, & Sparks, P. Highlighting relatedness promotes prosocial motives and behavior. *Personality* *and Social Psychology Bulletin 37, no. 7 (2011)*, 905-917; Dunn, E. & Norton, M. *Happy Money: The Science of Happier Spending*. Simon and Schuster, 2014.

Track Your Kindness... Otake, K., Shimai, S., Tanaka-Matsumi, J., Otsui, K. & Fredrickson, B. L. (2006). Happy people become happier through kindness: A counting kindnesses intervention. *Journal of Happiness Studies, 7*, 361-375.

Have A Kindness Day... Lyubomirsky, S. & Layous, K. (2013). How do simple positive activities increase well-being? *Current Directions in Psychological Science, 22(1)*, 57-62.

Try Loving-Kindness Meditation... Fredrickson, B. L., Cohn, M. A., Coffey, K. A., Pek, J. & Finkel, S. M. (2008). Open hearts build lives: Positive emotions, induced through loving-kindness meditation, build consequential personal resources. *Journal of Personality and Social Psychology, 95*, 1045-1062.

Studies suggest that people who are regularly grateful... Emmons, R.A. & Shelton, C.M. (2002). Gratitude and the science of positive psychology. In Snyder, C.R. & Lopez, S.J. (Eds.). *Handbook of Positive Psychology*. Oxford, UK: Oxford University Press.

Research has found that gratitude has two parts... Emmons, R.A. (2010). *Gratitude Works! A 21-Day Program for Creating Emotional Prosperity*. San Francisco: Jossey-Bass Publishing.

Count Your Blessings... Emmons, R. A. & McCullough, M. E. (2003). Counting blessings versus burdens: an experimental investigation of gratitude and subjective well-being in daily life. *Journal of Personality and Social Psychology, 84(2)*, 377.

Write A Gratitude Letter... Lyubomirsky, S. (2008). *The How of Happiness: A New Approach to Getting the Life You Want*. New York, NY: Penguin.

Carry A Gratitude Scrap... Achor, S. (2013). *Before Happiness: The 5 Hidden Keys to Achieving Success, Spreading Happiness, and Sustaining Positive Change*. New York: Crown Publishing.

By intentionally enjoying the good things in your life... Jose, P. E., Lim, B. T. & Bryant, F. B. (2012). Does savoring increase happiness? A daily diary study. *The Journal of Positive Psychology, 7(3)*, 176-187.

Researchers suggest you can extend the benefits of these emotions... Bryant, F. B., Chadwick, E. D. & Kluwe, K. (2011). Understanding the processes that regulate positive emotional experience: Unsolved problems and future directions for theory and research on savoring. *International Journal of Wellbeing, 1(1)*.

Immerse Yourself... Bryant, F. B. & Veroff, J. (2007). *Savoring: A New Model of Positive Experience.* Lawrence Erlbaum Associates Publishers.

Relive Peak Moments... Ben-Shahar, T. (2009). *Even Happier: A Gratitude Journal for Daily Joy.* New York, NY: McGraw-Hill Companies.

Savor Your Stories... Lambert, N.M., Gwinn, M., Baumeister, R., Strachman, A., Washburn, I.J., Gable, S.L. & Fincham, F.D. (2012). A boost of positive affect: the perks of sharing positive experiences. *Journal of Social and Personal Relationships, 30, (1),* 24-43.

Researchers have found that developing distress tolerance... Zvolensky, M. J., Bernstein, A. & Vujanovic, A. A. (Eds.). (2011). *Distress tolerance: Theory, Research, and Clinical Applications.* Guilford Press.

Studies suggest that you can build your confidence for distress tolerance by... Kashdan, T. & Biswas-Diener, R. (2014). *The Upside of Your Dark Side: Why Being Your Whole Self—Not Just Your "Good" Self—Drives Success and Fulfillment.* New York, NY: Penguin.

Name Your Emotions... McQuaid, M. (2017). Does The Future Feel Overwhelming? *Huffington Post,* retrieved from http://www.huffingtobuildnpost.com/michelle-mcquaid/does-the-future-feel-over_b_13886786.html

Slow Down Responses... Kassinove, H. & Tafrate, R. (2002). *Anger Management: The Complete Treatment Guidebook for Practitioners (Practical Therapist).* California: Impact Publishers.

Control The Controllables... Kashdan, T. & Biswas-Diener, R. (2014). *The Upside of Your Dark Side: Why Being Your Whole Self—Not Just Your "Good" Self—Drives Success and Fulfillment.* New York, NY: Penguin.

Research makes a distinction between a stressor... McGonigal, K. (2015). *The Upside of Stress: Why Stress Is Good for You and How to Get Good at It.* London, UK: Vermillion.

Seeing the good in stress doesn't require you to abandon your awareness... Crum, A. J., Salovey, P. & Achor, S. (2013). Rethinking stress: The role of mindsets in determining the stress response. *Journal of Personality and Social Psychology, 104*(4), 716.

Decode Stress Messages: McGonigal, K. (2015). *The Upside of Stress: Why Stress Is Good for You and How to Get Good at It.* London, UK: Vermillion.

Turn Adversity Into A Resource: Seery, M. D., Leo, R. J., Lupien, S. P., Kondrak, C. L. & Almonte, J. L. (2013). An upside to adversity? Moderate cumulative lifetime adversity is associated with resilient responses in the face of controlled stressors. *Psychological Science*, 0956797612469210.

Set Stretch Goals: McGonigal, K. (2015). *The Upside of Stress: Why Stress Is Good for You and How to Get Good at It.* London, UK: Vermillion.

Chapter 3: Enhancing Engagement

Professor Mihaly Csikszentmihalyi from Claremont Graduate University describes a state of high engagement as 'flow".... Csikszentmihalyi, M. (1990). *Flow: The Psychology of Optimal Experience.* New York, NY: Harper Perennial.

Researchers suggest that experiencing a state of flow comes with a host of benefits... Lyubomirsky, S. (2008). *The How of Happiness: A Scientific Approach to Getting the Life You Want.* New York, NY: Penguin.

Figuring out what your strengths are—those things you are good at and actually enjoy doing... Seligman, M. E. (2004). *Authentic Happiness: Using the New Positive Psychology to Realize Your Potential for Lasting Fulfillment.* New York, NY: Simon and Schuster.

But the key to consistently feeling engaged in what you're doing isn't simply to use your strengths more... Linley, P. A. (2008). *Average to A+: Realizing Strengths in Yourself and Others (Strengthing the World).*Coventry, UK: CAPP Press.

Developing your strengths allows you to work with the ways your brain is already wired to perform at its best... Buckingham, M. & Clifton, D. O. (2001). *Now, Discover Your Strengths.* New York, NY: Simon and Schuster.

Some researchers suggest that perhaps an eighty percent focus on developing your strengths... Cooperrider, D. L. & McQuaid, M. (2012). The Positive Arc of Systemic Strengths: How Appreciative Inquiry and Sustainable Designing Can Bring Out the Best in Human Systems. *Journal of Corporate Citizenship, 2012* (46), 71-102.

Studies find that when you have the opportunity to use your strengths... McQuaid, M. & Lawn, E. (2014). *Your Strengths Blueprint: How to be Engaged, Energized & Happy at Work.* Melbourne, Victoria: Michelle McQuaid Pty Ltd.

Researchers suggest the first step is to become aware... Niemiec, R.N. (2014). *Mindfulness and Character Strengths: A Practical Guide to Flourishing.* Boston, MA: Hogrefe Publishing.

Name Your Strengths... McQuaid, M. & Lawn, E. (2014). *Your Strengths Blueprint: How to be Engaged, Energized & Happy at Work.* Melbourne, Victoria: Michelle McQuaid Pty Ltd.

See Your Reflected Best Self... Roberts, L. M., Dutton, J. E., Spreitzer, G. M., Heaphy, E. D. & Quinn, R. E. (2005). Composing the reflected best-self portrait: Building pathways for becoming extraordinary in work organizations. *Academy of Management Review, 30*(4), 712-736.

Have A Daily Strengths Reflection... Niemiec, R.N. (2014). *Mindfulness and Character Strengths: A Practical Guide to Flourishing.* Boston, MA: Hogrefe Publishing.

Studies suggest that imagining what is possible triggers your brain's neural reward system... Cooperrider, D. L. (1990) Positive Image, Positive Action: The Affirmative Basis of Organizing. In Srivastava, S., Cooperrider, D.L. & associates (Eds) *Appreciative Management and Leadership.* San Francisco, CA: Jossey-Bass.

Researchers suggest that while your strengths exist within you and are a reflection of how your brain is wired to perform at its best... Peterson, C. & Seligman, M. E. (2004). *Character Strengths and Virtues: A Handbook and Classification.* Oxford University Press.

Studies have found this can build understanding of your motives... King, L. A. (2001). The health benefits of writing about life goals. *Personality and Social Psychology Bulletin, 27*(7), 798-807.

Meet Your Best Possible Self... King, L. A. (2001). The health benefits of writing about life goals. *Personality and Social Psychology Bulletin, 27*(7), 798-807.

Craft Your Job... Berg, J. M., Dutton, J. E. & Wrzesniewski, A. (2013). Job crafting and meaningful work. *Purpose and Meaning in the Workplace*, 81-104.

Create A ROAD MAP... Niemiec, R.N. (2014). *Mindfulness and Character Strengths: A Practical Guide to Flourishing.* Boston, MA: Hogrefe Publishing.

Studies suggest that small, regular actions are the best way to create lasting change... Heath, C. & Heath, D. (2010). *Switch: How to Change When Change Is Hard.* New York, NY: Random House.

Studies suggest that by mindfully focusing in an open, curious and nonjudgmental way... Niemiec, R.N. (2014). *Mindfulness and Character Strengths: A Practical Guide to Flourishing.* Boston, MA: Hogrefe Publishing.

Use Your Strengths In A New Way... Seligman, M. E., Steen, T. A., Park, N. & Peterson, C. (2005). Positive psychology progress: empirical validation of interventions. *American Psychologist, 60(5),* 410.

Take A Mindful Strengths Pause... Niemiec, R.N. (2014). *Mindfulness and Character Strengths: A Practical Guide to Flourishing.* Boston, MA: Hogrefe Publishing.

Invest In A Daily Strengths Habit... McQuaid, M. and Lawn, E. (2014). *Your Strengths Blueprint: How to be Engaged, Energized & Happy at Work.* Melbourne, Victoria: Michelle McQuaid Pty Ltd.

Studies have found that being mindful can help you... Langer, E. J. (1989). *Mindfulness.* New York, NY: Addison Wesley Longman.

Studies also suggest that mindfully focusing in an open, curious, and nonjudgmental... Langer, E. J. (2007). *On Becoming an Artist: Reinventing Yourself Through Mindful Creativity.* New York, NY: Ballantine Books.

Eat Mindfully... Tan, C. M. (2012). *Search Inside Yourself.* New York, NY: Harper Collins.

Look For What's Novel: Langer, E. J. (2007). *On Becoming an Artist: Reinventing Yourself Through Mindful Creativity.* Ballantine Books.

Embrace Not Knowing... Langer, E. J. (1989). *Mindfulness.* New York, NY: Addison Wesley Longman.

Researchers suggest that you are built to play and built through play... Brown, S. L. (2009). *Play: How it Shapes the Brain, Opens the Imagination, and Invigorates the Soul.* New York, NY: Penguin

Create Your Play History... Brown, S. L. (2009). *Play: How it Shapes the Brain, Opens the Imagination, and Invigorates the Soul.* New York, NY: Penguin.

Be Playful... Kane, P. (2004). *The Play Ethic.* London, UK: Pan.

Get Active... Brown, S. L. (2009). *Play: How it Shapes the Brain, Opens the Imagination, and Invigorates the Soul.* New York, NY: Penguin.

Try Rapidly Prototyping... Brown, T. & Wyatt, J. (2010). Design thinking for social innovation. *Development Outreach, 12*(1), 29-43.

Chapter 4: Nurturing Positive Relationships

One consistent finding to date... Peterson, C. (2006). *A Primer in Positive Psychology.* New York, NY: Oxford University Press.

A sense of belonging correlates with a range of positive outcomes... Smith, E. E. (2017). *The Power of Meaning: Crafting a Life That Matters.* New York, NY: Random House.

More than what you're doing at work, research suggests that it's who you're doing it with... Rath, T., Harter, J. K. & Harter, J. (2010). *Wellbeing: The Five Essential Pillars.* New York, NY: Simon and Schuster.

You have a biological need for social support... Fredrickson, B. (2013). *Love 2.0: How Our Supreme Emotion Affects Everything We Feel, Think, Do, and Become.* New York, NY: Hudson St Press.

In fact, studies have found that each positive interaction you have... Dutton, J. E. & Heaphy, E. D. (2003). The power of high-quality connections. *Positive organizational scholarship: Foundations of a new discipline, 3*, 263-278.

When you experience warm and trusting feelings toward another person... Fredrickson, B. (2013). *Love 2.0: How Our Supreme Emotion Affects Everything We Feel, Think, Do, and Become.* New York, NY: Hudson Street Press.

Professor Jane Dutton from the University of Michigan explains... Dutton, J. E. (2003). *Energize Your Workplace: How to Create and Sustain High-Quality Connections at Work* (Vol. 50). New York, NY: John Wiley & Sons.

It takes just a micro-moment of genuine connection to spark an upward spiral of mutual care... Fredrickson, B. (2013). *Love 2.0: How Our Supreme Emotion Affects Everything We Feel, Think, Do, and Become.* New York, NY: Hudson Street Press.

Christine Porath from Georgetown University has found that ninety-eight percent of people report experiencing uncivil... Porath, C. (2015). *Mastering Civility: A Manifesto for the Workplace.* New York, NY: Hachette Book Group.

A 2012 study by the Harvard School of Public Health... Slopen, N., Glynn, R. J., Buring, J. E., Lewis, T. T., Williams, D. R. & Albert, M. A. (2012). Job strain, job insecurity, and incident cardiovascular disease in the Women's Health Study: results from a 10-year prospective study. *PLoS One, 7*(7), e40512.

Professor Adam Grant from Wharton Business School and his colleagues have found that when employees invest in effective high-quality connections... Grant, A. (2013b). Givers take all: The hidden dimension of corporate culture. *McKinsey Quarterly,* 2, 52-65.

Researchers suggest that you can safely assume that there is pain in every room... Kanov, J. M., Maitlis, S., Worline, M. C., Dutton, J. E., Frost, P. J. & Lilius, J. M. (2004). Compassion in organizational life. *American Behavioral Scientist, 47*(6), 808-827.

Studies are finding that when you practice compassion... Worline, M.C. & Dutton, J.E. (2017.) *Awakening Compassion at Work: The Quiet Power That Elevates People and Organizations.* Oakland, CA: Berrett-Koehler Publishers, Inc.

Be Available... Worline, M.C. & Dutton, J.E. (2017) *Awakening Compassion at Work: The Quiet Power That Elevates People and Organizations.* Oakland, CA: Berrett-Koehler Publishers, Inc.

Listen Empathetically... Dutton, J. E., Workman, K. M. & Hardin, A. E. (2014). Compassion at work. *Annual Review Organizational Psychology Organizational Behavior 1*(1), 277-304.

Offer Micro-Moves... Worline, M.C. & Dutton, J.E. (2017). *Awakening Compassion at Work: The Quiet Power That Elevates People and Organizations.* Oakland, CA: Berrett-Koehler Publishers, Inc.

Studies have found that trust is fostered by acting with integrity, dependability and good motives... Lewecki, R.J. & Bunker, B.B. (1995). Developing and Maintaining Trust in Work Relationships. *Trust in Organizations.* In Kramer, R.M. & Tyler, T.R. (Eds.). Thousand Oaks, CA: Sage Publications.

Professor Jane Dutton, Monica Worline and their colleagues are finding that you can build trust by... Dutton, J. E. (2003). *Energize Your Workplace: How to Create and Sustain High-Quality Connections at Work* (Vol. 50). New York, NY: John Wiley & Sons.

Map Your Trust Bank... Dutton, J. E. (2003). *Energize Your Workplace: How to Create and Sustain High-Quality Connections at Work* (Vol. 50). New York, NY: John Wiley & Sons.

Give Away Control... Williams, M. (2001). *Seeing through the client's eyes: building interpersonal trust, cooperation and performance across organizational boundaries.* Unpublished doctoral dissertation, University of Michigan.

Ask for Input... Dutton, J. E. (2003). *Energize Your Workplace: How to Create and Sustain High-Quality Connections at Work* (Vol. 50). New York, NY: John Wiley & Sons.

Communicate Openly... Porath, C. (2015). *Mastering civility: A Manifesto for the Workplace.* New York, NY: Hachette Book Group.

A growing body of evidence suggests that they play as much of a role in your success as hard work... Grant, A. (2013). In the company of givers and takers. *Harvard Business Review, 91*(4), 90-97.

In giver mode, you look for ways... Grant, A. (2013). *Give and Take: A Revolutionary Approach to Success.* New York NY: Penguin.

Perform Five-Minute Favors... Grant, A. (2013). *Give and Take: A Revolutionary Approach to Success.* New York NY: Penguin.

Communicate Powerlessly... Hosman, L. (2015). Powerful and Powerless Speech Styles and Their Relationship to Perceived Dominance and Control. *The Exercise of Power in Communication: Devices, Reception and Reaction,* 221.

Chunk Your Giving... Grant, A. (2013). *Give and Take: A Revolutionary Approach to Success.* New York NY: Penguin.

Studies suggest, however, that learning to let go of grudges is likely to make you less hateful... McCullough, M. E. (2000). Forgiveness as human strength: Theory, measurement, and links to well-being. *Journal of Social and Clinical Psychology, 19*(1), 43-55.

Researchers recommend letting go of grudges by viewing the people who have wronged you with compassion... Bright, D.S. & Exline, J.J. (2012). Forgiveness at Four Levels: Intrapersonal, Relational, Organizational and Collective Group. *The Oxford Handbook of Positive Organizational Scholarship.* In Cameron, K.S. & Spreitzer, G.M. (Eds.). New York: Oxford University Press.

Find Meaning... McCullough, M., Root L. & Cohen A, (2006). Writing about the benefits of an interpersonal transgression facilitates forgiveness. *Journal of Consulting and Clinical Psychology, 74, (5),* 887-897.

Build Forgiveness Muscles... vanOyen Witvliet, C., DeYoung, N. J., Hofelich, A. J. & DeYoung, P. A. (2011). Compassionate reappraisal and emotion suppression as alternatives to offense-focused rumination: Implications for forgiveness and psychophysiological well-being. *The Journal of Positive Psychology, 6*(4), 286-299.

Show Mercy... McCullough, M. E. (2000). Forgiveness as human strength: Theory, measurement, and links to well-being. *Journal of Social and Clinical Psychology, 19*(1), 43-55.

Researchers have found that high-quality connections don't necessarily mean a deep or intimate relationship... Dutton, J. E. (2003). *Energize Your Workplace: How to Create and Sustain High-Quality Connections at Work* (Vol. 50). New York, NY: John Wiley & Sons.

Studies have found that you can nurture high-quality connections by engaging respectfully with others... Dutton, J. E. & Heaphy, E. D. (2003). The power of high-quality connections. *Positive organizational scholarship: Foundations of a new discipline, 3*, 263-278.

Ask Appreciative Questions... Dutton, J. E. (2003). *Energize Your Workplace: How to Create and Sustain High-Quality Connections at Work* (Vol. 50). New York, NY: John Wiley & Sons.

Prioritize Friendships... Rath, T. & Harter, J. K. (2010). *Wellbeing: The Five Essential Pillars*. Gallup Press.

Respond Actively And Constructively... Gable, S. L., Reis, H. T., Impett, E. A. & Asher, E. R. (2004). What do you do when things go right? The intrapersonal and interpersonal benefits of sharing positive events. *Journal of Personality and Social Psychology, 87*(2), 228.

Look For Strengths... McQuaid, M. and Lawn, E. (2014). *Your Strengths Blueprint: How to be Engaged, Energized & Happy at Work*. Melbourne, Victoria: Michelle McQuaid Pty Ltd.

Associate Professor Christine Porath suggests that incivility appears to be on the rise in our workplaces... Porath, C. & Pearson, C. (2013). The price of incivility. *Harvard Business Review, 91*(1-2), 114-121.

Researchers suggest it's important you don't let someone make you a smaller version of yourself... Porath, C. L. & Pearson, C. M. (2012). Emotional and behavioral responses to workplace incivility and the impact of hierarchical status. *Journal of Applied Social Psychology, 42*(S1), E326-E357.

Value Civility... Porath, C. (2015). *Mastering Civility: A Manifesto for the Workplace.* New York, NY: Hachette Book Group.

Take Control... Porath, C. (2016). Managing yourself an antidote to incivility. *Harvard Business Review, 94*(4), 108-111.

Gain Clarity... Porath, C. (2015). *Mastering Civility: A Manifesto for the Workplace.* New York, NY: Hachette Book Group.

Chapter 5: Finding More Meaning

For decades, people have ranked having a sense of purpose in their work... Cascio, W. F. (2003). Changes in workers, work, and organizations. *Handbook of Psychology.*

While researchers have noted that people struggle to find meaning in their jobs... Grant, A. (2014). The #1 Feature of Meaningless Work. *Huffington Post.* Retrieved from http://www.huffingtonpost.com/adamgrant/the-1-feature-of-a-meanin_b_4691464.html.

When a sense of meaning is found in our work, a growing body of evidence suggests... Steger, M. F. & Dik, B. J. (2010). Work as meaning: Individual and organizational benefits of engaging in meaningful work. In Linley, P.A., Harrington, S. & Page, N. (Eds.). *Oxford Handbook of Positive Psychology and Work,* (pp 131 – 142). Oxford, UK: Oxford University Press.

Researcher Emily Esfahni Smith suggests... Smith, E. E. (2017). *The Power of Meaning: Crafting a Life That Matters.* New York, NY: Random House.

Instead, studies suggest your sense of meaning usually unfolds bit by bit... Duckworth, A. (2016). *Grit: The Power of Passion and Perseverance.* New York, NY: Simon and Schuster.

Angela Duckworth from the University of Pennsylvania suggests that if you haven't found your passion yet... Duckworth, A. (2016). *Grit: The Power of Passion and Perseverance.* New York, NY: Simon and Schuster.

According to Professor Bill Damon at Stanford University, your interests are the sparks... Damon, W. (2009). *The Path to Purpose: How Young People Find Their Calling in Life.* New York, NY: Free Press.

Professor Amy Wrzesniewski from Yale University has found that no matter what your job description says... Wrzesniewski, A., LoBuglio, N., Dutton, J. E. & Berg, J. M. (2013). Job crafting and cultivating positive meaning and identity in work. *Advances in Positive Organizational Psychology* (pp. 281-302). Emerald Group Publishing Limited.

Professor Robert Vallerand, from the Universite du Quebec a Montreal, has found that our passions can be either harmonious or obsessive... Vallerand, R. J. & Houlfort, N. (2003). Passion at work. *Emerging Perspectives on Values in Organizations*, 175-204.

Researchers are finding that we all need to feel understood, recognized, and affirmed by others... Smith, E. E. (2017). *The Power of Meaning: Crafting a Life That Matters*. New York, NY: Random House.

Researchers suggest that belonging is more likely to occur when your relationships... Baumeister, R.F. & Leary, M.R. (1995). The need to belong: desire for interpersonal attachments as a fundamental human motivation. *Psychological Bulletin, 117*(3), 497 – 529.

Give At Work... Grant, A. (2013). *Give and Take: A Revolutionary Approach to Success.* New York NY: Penguin.

Find Your Tribe... Smith, E. E. (2017). *The Power of Meaning: Crafting a Life That Matters.* New York, NY: Random House.

See Others... Porath, C. (2015) *Mastering Civility: A Manifesto for the Workplace.* New York, NY: Hachette Book Group.

Studies have found you'll be more motivated to accomplish the goals that matter most to you... Smith, E. E. (2017). *The Power of Meaning: Crafting a Life That Matters*. New York, NY: Random House.

Researchers suggest that instead of approaching your purpose as a noun... Rockind, C. L. (2011). Living on purpose: Why purpose matters and how to find it (Unpublished thesis). *Masters of Applied Positive Psychology Program.* The University of Pennsylvania, Philadelphia, PA.

For the Sake Of What?... Warrell, M. (2013.) *Stop Playing Safe: Rethink Risk, Unlock the Power of Courage, Achieve Outstanding Success.* Queensland, Australia: John Wiley & Sons Australia Ltd.

Make The Mundane Meaningful... Ben-Shahar, T. (2007). *Happier: Learn the Secrets to Daily Joy and Lasting Fulfillment.* New York, NY: McGraw-Hill Companies.

Invest In SPIRE... Steger, M.F. (2017). Creating meaning and purpose at work. In Oades, L.G., Steger, M., Delle-Fave, A. & Passmore, J. (Eds.). *The Wiley Blackwell Handbook of the Psychology of Positivity and Strengths-Based Approaches at Work*. Chichester: Wiley-Blackwell.

Outsource Inspiration... Grant, A. M., Campbell, E. M., Chen, G., Cottone, K., Lapedis, D. & Lee, K. (2007). Impact and the art of motivation maintenance: The effects of contact with beneficiaries on persistence behavior. *Organizational Behavior and Human Decision Processes, 103*(1), 53-67.

Researchers have found that people living meaningful lives... McAdams, D. P. (2013). The positive psychology of adult generativity: Caring for the next generation and constructing a redemptive life. *Positive Psychology* (pp. 191-205). Springer New York.

Studies have found that even making small story edits can have a big impact... Smith, E. E. (2017). *The Power of Meaning: Crafting a Life That Matters*. New York, NY: Random House.

Uncover Your Story... Pennebaker, J. W. (2004). *Writing to Heal: A guided journal for recovering from trauma and emotional upheaval*. New Harbinger Publisher.

Be A Journalist... McGonigal, K. (2015). *The Upside of Stress: Why Stress Is Good for You and How to Get Good at It*. London, UK: Vermillion.

Release Your Lost Self... King, L.A. & Hicks, J.A. (2007). Whatever happened to what might have been? Regrets, happiness and maturity. *American Psychological Association, 62(7)*, 625–636

Researchers have found that transcendent states occur when your sense of self washes away... Smith, E. E. (2017). *The Power of Meaning: Crafting a Life That Matters*. New York, NY: Random House.

Studies suggest that transcendence is enabled by experiencing the state of awe... Piff, P.K., Dietze, P., Feinberg, M., Stancato, D.M. & Keltner, D. (2015). Awe, the small self, and prosocial behavior. *Journal of Personality and Social Psychology, 108, (6)*, 883-899.

Be Awed By Nature... Zhang J. W., Piff P. K., Iyer R., Koleva S. & Keltner D. (2014). An occasion for unselfing: Beautiful nature leads to prosociality. *Journal of Environmental Psychology, 37*, 61–72.

Find A Spiritual Practice... Smith, E. E. (2017*). The Power of Meaning: Crafting a Life That Matters.* New York, NY: Random House.

Get Perspective... Smith, E. E. (2017). *The Power of Meaning: Crafting a Life That Matters.* New York, NY: Random House.

Researchers have found that while an obsessive passion is unlikely to do much damage in the short-term... Vallerand, R. J. & Houlfort, N. (2003). Passion at work. *Emerging Perspectives on Values in Organizations,* 175-204.

Restore Balance... McQuaid, M. (2017). Could Loving What You Do Be A Problem? *Huffington Post.* Retrieved from http://www.huffingtonpost.com/michelle-mcquaid/could-loving-what-you-do-_b_10874430.html

Cultivate Alternative Passions... Kaufman, S.B. (2011). Increase your passion for work without becoming obsessed. *Harvard Business Review.* Retrieved from https://hbr.org/2011/09/increase-your-passion-for-work

Set Boundaries... Vallerand, R. J., Houlfort, N. & Forest, J. (2014). Passion for work: Determinants and outcomes. *Oxford Handbook of Work Engagement, Motivation, and Self-Determination Theory,* 85-105.

Chapter 6: Amplifying Accomplishment

Professor Carol Dweck of Stanford University suggests that when it comes to accomplishing the things that matter most to you... Dweck, C. (2006). *Mindset: The New Psychology of Success.* New York, NY: Random House.

In one study of competitive swimmers, the very best performances... Chambliss, D. F. (1989). The mundanity of excellence: An ethnographic report on stratification and Olympic swimmers. *Sociological theory, 7*(1), 70-86.

Professor Angela Duckworth at the University of Pennsylvania explains that we tend to carry a hidden prejudice... Duckworth, A. (2016). *Grit: The Power of Passion and Perseverance.* New York, NY: Simon and Schuster. Tsay, Chia-Jung. (2016). "Privileging naturals over strivers: The costs of the naturalness bias." Personality and Social Psychology Bulletin 42, no. 1: 40-53.

Studies have found that a growth mindset makes it easier to set yourself stretch goals... Dweck, C. (2006). *Mindset: The New Psychology of Success.* New York, NY: Random House.

Author Caroline Adams Miller writes of "stupid grit"... Miller, C.A. (2017). *Getting Grit: The Evidence-Based Approach to Cultivating Passion, Perseverance, and Purpose.* Boulder, CO: Sounds True.

Dweck recently told us that a growth mindset can go wrong when... McQuaid, M. (2017). Are You Getting Growth Mindset Wrong? *Huffington Post.* Retrieved from http://www.huffingtonpost.com/entry/are-you-getting-growth-mindset-wrong_us_59310062e4b0649fff2117d3

Dr. Kristen Neff explains that when your efforts to learn and accomplish the things that matter most to you don't go as planned... Neff, K. D. & Dahm, K. A. (2015). Self-Compassion: What It Is, What It Does, and How It Relates to Mindfulness. In *Handbook of Mindfulness and Self-Regulation* (pp. 121-137). New York, NY: Springer.

Researchers have found that goals can provide you with motivation ... Locke, E. A. & Latham, G. P. (2002). Building a practically useful theory of goal setting and task motivation: A 35-year odyssey. *American Psychologist, 57*(9), 705.

Researchers suggest it should pass the "so what?" test... Miller, C.A. (2017). *Getting Grit: The Evidence-Based Approach to Cultivating Passion, Perseverance, and Purpose.* Boulder, CO: Sounds True.

Know What You Want... Ben-Shahar, T. (2007). *Happier: Learn the Secrets to Daily Joy and Lasting Fulfillment.* New York, NY: McGraw-Hill Companies.

Audit Your Time... Ben-Shahar, T. (2009). *Even Happier: A Gratitude Journal for Daily Joy.* New York, NY:McGraw-Hill Companies.

Stretch Yourself... Miller, C.A. (2017). *Getting Grit: The Evidence-Based Approach to Cultivating Passion, Perseverance, and Purpose.* Boulder, CO: Sounds True.

You have what researchers define as hope... Lopez, S. J. (2013). *Making Hope Happen: Create the Future You Want for Yourself and Others.* New York, NY: Simon and Schuster.

Researchers suggest that hope isn't innate, nor a by-product of your IQ... Snyder, C. R. (Ed.). (2000). *Handbook of Hope: Theory, Measures, and Applications.* Orlando, FL: Academic Press.

Map Your Hopes... Lopez, S. J. (2013). *Making Hope Happen: Create the Future You Want for Yourself and Others.* New York, NY: Simon and Schuster.

Start A Passion Project... McQuaid, M. (2015). What Sets the Most Successful Managers Apart? *Huffington Post.* Retrieved from http://www.huffingtonpost.com/michelle-mcquaid/what-sets-the-most-succes_b_6626868.html

Nobel Prize winners are twenty-two times more likely to perform as actors, dancers, or magicians... Grant, A. (2016). How to Raise a Creative Child. *New York Times.* Retrieved from https://www.nytimes.com/2016/01/31/opinion/sunday/how-to-raise-a-creative-child-step-one-back-off.html?mcubz=2.

Find Hopeful Friends... Lopez, S. J. (2013). *Making Hope Happen: Create the Future You Want for Yourself and Others.* New York, NY: Simon and Schuster.

Researchers have found this response is often the result of a "fixed mindset"... Dweck, C. (2006). *Mindset: The New Psychology of Success.* New York, NY: Random House.

Set Learning Goals... Dweck, C. (2006). *Mindset: The New Psychology of Success.* New York, NY: Random House.

Get Comfortable With Failure... McQuaid, M. (2017). Are You Getting Growth Mindset Wrong? *Huffington Post.* Retrieved from http://www.huffingtonpost.com/entry/are-you-getting-growth-mindset-wrong_us_59310062e4b0649fff2117d3

Name Your Fixed Mindset... McQuaid, M. (2017). Are You Getting Growth Mindset Wrong? *Huffington Post.* Retrieved from http://www.huffingtonpost.com/entry/are-you-getting-growth-mindset-wrong_us_59310062e4b0649fff2117d3

Yet researchers have suggested that grit is a key predictor of success... Duckworth, A. (2016). *Grit: The Power of Passion and Perseverance.* New York, NY: Simon and Schuster.

Researchers suggest that it can help to set meaningful goals... Eskreis-Winkler, L., Gross, J. J. & Duckworth, A. L. (in press). Grit: Sustained self-regulation in the service of superordinate goals. In K. D. Vohs & R. F. Baumeister (Eds.), *Handbook of Self-Regulation: Research, Theory and Applications* (3rd ed.). New York, NY: Guilford

Draw A Grit Map... Duckworth, A. (2016). *Grit: The Power of Passion and Perseverance.* New York, NY: Simon and Schuster.

Ask For Help... Miller, C.A. (2017). *Getting Grit: The Evidence-Based Approach to Cultivating Passion, Perseverance, and Purpose.* Boulder, CO: Sounds True.

Invest In Deliberate Practice... Ericsson, K. A., Krampe, R. T. & Tesch-Römer, C. (1993). The role of deliberate practice in the acquisition of expert performance. *Psychological Review, 100*(3), 363.

Researchers suggest that confidence is your ability to turn your thoughts into action... Kay, K. & Shipman, C. (2014). *The Confidence Code: The Science and Art of Self-Assurance-What Women Should Know.* New York, NY: Harper Collins.

Take One Small Step... Kay, K. & Shipman, C. (2014). *The Confidence Code: The Science and Art of Self-Assurance-What Women Should Know.* New York, NY: Harper Collins.

Acknowledge "Not Yet"... Dweck, C. (2014). The power of believing that you can improve. *TED Talk.* Transcript and video available: https://www. ted. com/talks/carol_dweck_the_power_of_believing_that_you_ can_improve/transcript.

Strike A Power Pose... Carney, D., Cuddy, A. J. C., & Yap, A. (2010). Power posing: Brief nonverbal displays affect neuroendocrine levels and risk tolerance. *Psychological Science Online,* 1363-1368.

Researchers have found that for many of us, self-criticism is our first response as our brain tries to protect us... Neff, K. (2003). Self-compassion: An alternative conceptualization of a healthy attitude toward oneself. *Self and Identity, 2*(2), 85-101.

Researchers suggest that there are three practices that can cultivate self-compassion... Neff, K. D. (2011). Self-compassion, self-esteem, and well-being. *Social and Personality Psychology Compass, 5*(1), 1-12.

Create A Mantra... Neff, K. (2011). *Self-Compassion. The Proven Power of Being Kind to Yourself.* New York, NY: Harper Collins.

Write A Letter... Shapira, L. & Mongrain, M. (2010). The benefits of self-compassion and optimism exercises for individuals vulnerable to depression. *The Journal of Positive Psychology, 5(5),* 377-389.

Soothe Your Pain... Neff, K. (2011). *Self-Compassion. The Proven Power of Being Kind to Yourself.* New York, NY: Harper Collins.

Researchers have found that when you experience adversity or trauma... Bonanno, G. A. (2004). Loss, trauma, and human resilience: have we underestimated the human capacity to thrive after extremely aversive events? *American Psychologist, 59*(1), 20.

Studies suggest that themes of personalization... Seligman, M.E.P. (1990). *Learned Optimism: How to Change Your Mind and Your Life.* New York, NY: Vintage Books.

Researchers also suggest it can be helpful to tune into the stories you're telling yourself... Reivich, K. & Shatté, A. (2002). *The Resilience Factor: 7 Essential Skills for Overcoming Life's Inevitable Obstacles.* New York, NY: Broadway Books.

Challenge Your Beliefs... Seligman, M.E.P. (1990). *Learned Optimism: How to Change Your Mind and Your Life.* New York, NY: Vintage Books.

Lean Into The Suck... Sandberg, S. & Grant, A. (2017). *Option B: Facing Adversity, Building Resilience and Finding Joy.* New York, NY: Random House.

Ban "Always"... Reivich, K. & Shatté, A. (2002). *The Resilience Factor: 7 Essential Skills for Overcoming Life's Inevitable Obstacles.* New York, NY: Broadway Books.

Flex Your Stress Mindset... McGonigal, K. (2015). *The Upside of Stress: Why Stress Is Good for You and How to Get Good at It.* London, UK: Vermillion.

Chapter 7: Heightening Health

Considerable research has focused on how to support good physical health... Kern, M. L. (2016). Exercise, physical activity, and mental health. In Friedman, H.S. (Ed.), *Encyclopedia of Mental Health* (2nd Ed., Vol 2, pp. 175-180). Waltham, MA: Academic Press.

Researchers suggest that we tend to be lousy judges of how much looking after our body impacts our performance and our wellbeing... Rath, T. (2013). *Eat, Move, Sleep: How Small Choices Lead to Big Changes.* New York, NY: Missionday, LLC.

Harvard sleep expert, Charles Czeisler, wrote... Buxton, O. M., Cain, S. W., O'Connor, S. P., Porter, J. H., Duffy, J. F., Wang, W., Czeisler, C.A. & Shea, S. A. (2012). Adverse metabolic consequences in humans of prolonged sleep restriction combined with circadian disruption. *Science Translational Medicine, 4*(129), 129ra43-129ra43.

Foods like pasta, bread, cereal, and soda release their glucose quickly... Murphy, K. (2016). A Personalized Diet, Better Suited to You. *New York Times.* Retrieved from http://well.blogs.nytimes.com/2016/01/11/apersonalized-diet-better-suited-to-you/?_r=0.

Declared the most underrated health threat of our time... Hellmich, N. (2012, August 13). Take a stand against sitting disease. *USA Today.* Retrieved from http://www.usatoday.com/news/health/story/2012-07-19/sitting-disease-questionsanswers/ 57016756/1.

Researchers suggest that ninety-five percent of us need somewhere between seven and nine hours of sleep... Jones, M. (2011, April 15). How Little Sleep Can You Get Away With? *The New York Times.* Retrieved from http://www.nytimes.com/2011/04/17magazine/mag-17Sleep-t.html

Studies suggest that your body will run best on a twenty-four-hour schedule... Stuster, J. (2011). *Bold Endeavors: Lessons from Polar and Space Exploration.* Naval Institute Press.

Researchers suggest that one way to ensure you're getting enough sleep is to have a bedtime routine... Rath, T. (2013). *Eat, Move, Sleep: How Small Choices Lead to Big Changes.* New York, NY: Missionday, LLC.

Forgo Sleep Ins... Stuster, J. (2011). *Bold Endeavors: Lessons from Polar and Space Exploration.* Naval Institute Press.

Create Bedtime Routines... Schwartz, T. (2011). Sleep is More Important than Food. *Harvard Business Review.* Retrieved from https://hbr.org/2011/03/sleep-is-more-important-than-f/; Barker, E. (2015). Get Better Sleep: 5 Powerful New Tips From Research. *Time Magazine.* Retrieved from http://time.com/3942487/better-sleep-tips-research/.

Toss The Turning... Rath, T. (2013). *Eat, Move, Sleep: How Small Choices Lead to Big Changes.* New York, NY: Missionday, LLC.

Researchers suggest that it may be helpful to start thinking about food not as calories, but as energy... Rath, T. (2013). *Eat, Move, Sleep: How Small Choices Lead to Big Changes.* New York, NY: Missionday, LLC.

Plan Your Diet... Friedman, R. (2014). What You Eat Affects Your Productivity. *Harvard Business Review.* Retrieved from https://hbr.org/2014/10/what-you-eataffects-your-productivity/

Eat Small Meals Frequently... Murphy, K.(2016). A Personalized Diet, Better Suited To You. *New York Times.* Retrieved from http://well.blogs.nytimes.com/2016/01/11/apersonalized-diet-better-suited-to-you/?_r=0.

Track And Adjust... Rath, T. (2013). *Eat, Move, Sleep: How Small Choices Lead to Big Changes.* New York, NY: Missionday, LLC.

Researchers suggest that while thirty minutes of physical activity, five times a week... American Heart Association (2015). *American Heart Association's recommended physical activity in Adults.* Retrieved from http://www.heart.org/HEARTORG/GettingHealthy/PhysicalActivity/FitnessBasics/American-Heart-Association-Recommendations-for-Physical-Activity-in-Adults_UCM_307976_Article.jsp#.VkqwPoRWj8k

Studies suggest that regular physical activity and exercise helps prevent and manage physical illness... Rath, T. (2013). *Eat, Move, Sleep: How Small Choices Lead to Big Changes.* New York, NY: Missionday.

Studies have found that there are hundreds of moments in a typical day where you can embed extra activity in your routine... Doheny, K. (2009, May 29). Post-Exercise 'Glow' May Last 12 Hours. *US News and World Report.* Retrieved from http://health. usnews.com/healthnews/family-health/brain-and-behavior/articles/2009/05/29/post-exercise-glow-may-last-12-hours; Khan, A. (2015). Easy Ways to Get 10,000 Steps Per Day. *US News.* Retrieved from http://health.usnews.com/health-news/health-wellness/slideshows/easy-ways-to-get-10-000-steps-per-day.

Count Your Steps... Bravata, D. M., Smith-Spangler, C., Sundaram, V., Gienger, A. L., Lin, N., Lewis, R., Stave, C. D., Olkin, I. & Sirard, J. R. (2007). Using pedometers to increase physical activity and improve health: A systematic review. *Journal of the American Medical Association,* 298(19), 2296–2304. doi:10.1001/jama.298.19.2296

Get Up Regularly... Rath, T. (2013). *Eat, Move, Sleep: How Small Choices Lead to Big Changes.* New York, NY: Missionday;

Start Early... Post-Exercise 'Glow' May Last 12 Hours. *US News and World Report.* Retrieved from http://health.usnews.com/healthnews/family-health/brain-and-behavior/articles/2009/05/29/post-exercise-glow-may-last-12-hours

Move At Home... Thomas, J. G., Bond, D. S., Hill, J. O. & Wing, R. R. (2011). The National Weight Control Registry: A Study of "Successful Losers". *ACSM's Health & Fitness Journal,* 15(2), 8-12.

Yet, researchers have found that when you expend too much energy without sufficient recovery periods... Loehr, J., Loehr, J. E. & Schwartz, T. (2005). *The Power of Full Engagement: Managing Energy, Not Time, Is the Key to High Performance and Personal Renewal.* New York, NY: Simon and Schuster.

Just Be... Farhi, D. (1996). *The Breathing Book: Good Health and Vitality Through Essential Breath Work.* New York, NY: Macmillan.

Mindfully Meditate... Tan, C. M. (2012). *Search Inside Yourself: Increase Productivity, Creativity and Happiness.* New York, NY: HarperCollins.

Create A Third Space... Fraser, A. (2012). *The Third Space: Using Life's Little Transitions to Find Balance and Happiness.* Sydney, Australia: William Heinemann, Australia.

Chapter 8: Maintaining Your Wellbeing

Researchers have found that much of your behavior is contagious... Fowler, J. H. & Christakis, N. A. (2008). Dynamic spread of happiness in a large social network: longitudinal analysis over 20 years in the Framingham Heart Study. *Bmj, 337,* a2338.

About The Authors

About Michelle McQuaid

Michelle McQuaid is a best-selling author, workplace wellbeing teacher, and playful change activator. With more than a decade of senior leadership experience in large organizations around the world, she's passionate about translating cutting-edge research from positive psychology and neuroscience, into practical strategies for health, happiness, and business success.

An honorary fellow at Melbourne University's Graduate School of Education, she blogs for Psychology Today, Huffington Post and Live Happy, and her work has been featured in *Forbes*, the *Harvard Business Review*, *The Wall Street Journal*, *Boss Magazine*, *The Age* and more.

She holds a Masters in Applied Positive Psychology from the University of Pennsylvania and is currently completing her PhD in Appreciative Inquiry under the supervision of David Cooperrider.

Michelle lives to help people discover their strengths, move beyond their fears, and finally discover what it truly takes to flourish with confidence. You can find more of Michelle's work at **www.michellemcquaid.com**.

About Peggy Kern

Dr. Peggy Kern is a senior lecturer at the Centre for Positive Psychology within The University of Melbourne's Graduate School of Education. Originally trained in social, personality, and developmental psychology, Peggy received her undergraduate degree from Arizona State University, a Masters and PhD in social/personality psychology from the University of California, Riverside, and postdoctoral training from the University of Pennsylvania. She has worked directly with many of the leaders in positive psychology, including Martin Seligman, Angela Duckworth, James Pawelski, George Vaillant, Sonja Lyubomirsky, and Felicia Huppert, among others.

Her research focuses on understanding, measuring, and supporting wellbeing across the lifespan. She incorporates a lifespan perspective, mixed methodologies, and interdisciplinary collaboration. She works with schools and workplaces, and considers strategies for bridging gaps between research and practice. She has published more than fifty peer-reviewed articles and chapters. You can find out more about Peggy's work at **www.peggykern.org**.

Made in the USA
Monee, IL
21 April 2020

26497074R00108